TOMMIES

D1332460

Casemate Short History

TOMMIES

THE BRITISH ARMY
IN THE TRENCHES

Rosie Serdiville & John Sadler

CASEMATE
Oxford & Philadelphia

This one is for all of them who have
no known grave

Published in Great Britain and
the United States of America in 2017 by
CASEMATE PUBLISHERS
The Old Music Hall, 106–108 Cowley Road, Oxford OX4 1JE, UK and
1950 Lawrence Road, Havertown, PA 19083, USA

© Casemate Publishers 2017

Paperback Edition: ISBN 978-1-61200-484-6
Digital Edition: ISBN 978-1-61200-485-3

A CIP record for this book is available from the British Library

Maps by Chloe Rodham

Printed in the Czech Republic by FINIDR, s.r.o.

For a complete list of Casemate titles, please contact:

CASEMATE PUBLISHERS (UK)
Telephone (01865) 241249
Email: casemate-uk@casematepublishers.co.uk
www.casematepublishers.co.uk

CASEMATE PUBLISHERS (US)
Telephone (610) 853-9131
Fax (610) 853-9146
Email: casemate@casematepublishers.com
www.casematepublishers.com

CONTENTS

Introduction: When the Drums Begin to Roll…   7

Timeline   24

Abbreviations   26

Uniforms and kit   27

Chapter 1:   Deadlock (1914)   31

Chapter 2:   Stalemate (1915)   53

Chapter 3:   Attrition (1916)   76

Chapter 4:   Mud (1917)   95

Chapter 5:   Breakthrough (1918)   118

Chapter 6:   Remembrance   140

Sources   153

Acknowledgements   155

Yes, makin' mock o' uniforms that guard you while you sleep
Is cheaper than them uniforms, an' they're starvation cheap.
An' hustlin' drunken soldiers when they're goin' large a bit
Is five times better business than paradin' in full kit.
Then it's Tommy this, an' Tommy that, an' 'Tommy, 'ow's yer soul?'
But it's 'Thin red line of 'eroes' when the drums begin to roll
The drums begin to roll, my boys, the drums begin to roll,
O it's 'Thin red line of 'eroes,' when the drums begin to roll.

Rudyard Kipling, *Tommy Atkins*

INTRODUCTION

WHEN THE DRUMS BEGIN TO ROLL...

As sure as God's in his heaven,
As sure as he stands for right,
As sure as the Hun this wrong hath done,
So surely we win this fight!

John Oxenham, *Victory Day – Anticipation*

ON THE SULTRY AFTERNOON OF 28 JUNE 1914, an eighteen-year-old tubercular terrorist shot Archduke Franz Ferdinand and his wife outside a pavement cafe in the Bosnian city of Sarajevo. Few in Britain at that time had heard of the Duke, the city or the province and, for the most part, cared rather less; just another 'Balkan do'. It wasn't. This was the spark that lit the world; that blew the fuse that consumed the great empires and dynasties of Europe. Austria-Hungary, Germany, Russia and Turkey would be blown clear away. Britain was swept up in a tidal wave of righteous sentiment. The beastly Hun had to be stopped and gallant little Belgium restored. No other nation sustained its initial war effort entirely with volunteers. The posters let every man know what path duty demanded he take.

A call to arms

In that final, glorious summer of peace when it seemed the Empire was at its height and the King Emperor firmly on the throne, Britain stood tall as the world's only global superpower. Her navy had ruled the waves for over a century since Trafalgar. Atlases of the day showed significant tracts of the globe shaded in red. As an instrument of imperial policy, beside the Navy, stood Tommy Atkins, the private soldier. Generally he was not well liked though, as the Kipling poem suggests, he would be lauded and cheered as he went off to die for king and country. When and if he came back he was became invisible. This contemptuous view of redcoats didn't begin to change until the Crimean War (1854–56). Technology, in the form of the wireless telegraph, early battlefield photography and what would now be termed 'embedded' journalists meant Victorians in their comfortable parlours could fully witness all the horrors troops were suffering in the bleak Russian winter. Their privations were caused far more by supply and procurement failures than enemy action. Tommy won all his battles but froze thanks to the failures of the commissariat. Change was demanded; soldiers needed better care, decent accommodation and education. Change was, however, slow.

One of Marlborough's footsloggers toiling on the road to Blenheim in 1704 might have had little or no difficulty in recognising his great-grandson marching in the rain towards the ridge of Mont St. Jean under Wellington over a century later. Both wore the famous red coat. They marched or rode as armies had through distant centuries. They wheeled and drilled, delivered their platoon volleys in a very similar manner. Both carried a smoothbore flintlock musket that might just kill their man at fifty yards. Wellington's infantryman might have had far greater difficulty in recognising his own great-grandson, trudging along the hot pavé towards Mons in 1914. 'Tommy' was clad in stiff khaki. He carried the SMLE bolt action repeating rifle, deadly at a dozen times the distance of its predecessor. Much of his travel was undertaken by rail and the ubiquitous tin meant he could fight all year round and still be fed. None of this promised an easier life. Indeed his would very likely be harder, more terrifying and very much shorter.

The war had been a long time brewing. Seeds of conflict had been sown over forty years before when Prussia, burgeoning into a united Germany, trampled France, humiliatingly, unexpectedly and comprehensively, relieved her of both Alsace and Lorraine. Desire for revenge, *La Revanche*, burned fiercely in the breast of every Frenchman. In the course of those four decades, Imperial Germany – which had come late to the idea of nationalism and the scramble for empire – blossomed and boomed. Her industry came to rival that of Britain. Once the canny touch of the ageing Bismarck had been prised free, Kaiser Wilhelm II and his generation of gilded hawks, flushed with power and might, steamed headlong into fresh confrontation and hostility

The **Short Magazine Lee Enfield (SMLE)** was the standard British service rifle of the era: called 'short' because the barrel length was less than the earlier 'Long' Lee-Enfield which did service in the Boer War and still armed many territorial units in 1914. The SMLE was intended both for cavalry and infantry, firing 10 rounds of .303 ball cartridge. The weapon reached its final pre-war variant, the Mark III, in 1907 and confounded its critics, doing good service throughout the conflict and, depending on circumstances, for decades afterwards.

with Austria was forgotten as France and Russia drew together. This was ominous; a war on two fronts, east and west, was not to Germany's advantage.

If Germany had to fight on both flanks, she must deal swiftly with one opponent to then concentrate upon the other. Russia was the larger demon, with potential armies of millions. Count von Schlieffen gave his name to a strategic plan which proposed an immediate knockout blow in the west to deal swiftly with France before concentrating upon Russia, perceived as far slower to mobilise. Russia was industrialising fast. The German General Staff feared that, by 1917, her capacity would have expanded so prodigiously as to remove any prospect of victory. The whole European polity, by summer 1914 was a tinderbox, requiring only a single spark.

The killing of Franz Ferdinand inspired little mourning at home. Indeed conspiracy theorists might suggest his death was precisely what had been hoped for to provide a cast iron casus belli. There comes a point when the slide into war cannot be halted. A departed troop train, having departed, cannot be recalled. He who mobilises fastest can land the first, very probably decisive, blow. High command cannot simply wait upon events and hope for a diplomatic outcome. If one side begins to mobilise, the other must do likewise or else be left hopelessly exposed. Vast conscript armies cannot be summoned and marshalled overnight.

The opening battles in which the British Expeditionary Force (BEF) was pitched against enormous odds were fought at Mons

The **Quick-Firer** was an artillery innovation from the 1890s, distinguished from earlier ordnance in that they were fitted with buffers to limit recoil; the breech was adapted to allow rapid re-loading with shell and propellant combined in cartridge form. Consequently, in the early 20th century, the killing power or artillery increased exponentially.

and Le Cateau in a fast-moving war of manoeuvre. Wrong-footed and exposed, the BEF fought some masterly, if costly, actions and played its part in General Joffre's counterstroke on the Marne. From there they advanced into Belgium in what would become known as 'the Race for the Sea' which ended in the ferocity of First Ypres in October. This battle and those of 1915 drastically reduced the ranks of regular formations and handed the baton, in part, to Kitchener's 'New Service' Battalions.

After stalemate in 1915, came the colossal slaughter at Verdun and then the Somme, a battle that cost Britain and the Empire more dead than the entire course of World War II. In 1917 the British learnt how to crack the linear German defences and scored some great successes before German resilience and new defensive systems drowned all hopes in Flanders mud. For spring 1918, the Kaiser's generals unleashed a series of blistering offensives which came close to breaking the Allied line. Close but not close enough: the tide inexorably turned, victory won at enormous cost.

New small arms, accurate and deadly, were not the only lethal hazards on the battlefield. Field guns were quick firers, throwing high explosive shells over long distances with fearful accuracy. Hiram Maxim had heeded a colleague's exhortation that, if he wanted to make money, he should enable European armies to slaughter each other with greater ease. He obliged and the machine gun, with a range of 2,000 yards (1,829 metres), firing some 600 rounds per minute, would change the nature of the battlefield forever.

Mr Atkins

On 16 August 1819, British cavalry turned their sabres against protestors and put numerous of them ruthlessly to the sword. The Peterloo Massacre outraged public opinion. Yet it left men of property fearful that revolutionary trends were undermining the fabric of society, threatening to shake the established, God-given order of things. Something had to be done.

Raising local mounted forces, drawn from the tenantry and affinities of local magnates, landed and industrial, was considered the best means whereby those of substance might 'render effectual aid to the civil power in case of disturbance'. The Duke of Northumberland, a man of very great estate, called a meeting of county magistrates in October 1819. Within two months, the Northumberland and Newcastle Volunteer Corps of Cavalry was raised. For the most part, it comprised 'gentlemen of great respectability, such as merchants, brokers and tradesmen, together with officials of the collieries, and tenantry and retainers of the landed proprietors.'

For obvious reasons the Yeomanry were regarded as tools of oppression and these well-groomed class-warriors were soon dubbed 'the Noodles'. Oddly, in mining areas of Northumberland, everyday colliers volunteered, if they could afford it. The lure of working with horses outweighed disaffection. Indeed, the Ashington troop was soon amongst the smartest. There was stiff competition, gentlemen need to dress up. With their smart, tailored uniforms, they took on a very dandified air. Besides, if this was training for war, it smacked of romance and derring-do, of stiff parades 'of jewelled hilts/ for daggers in plaid socks; of smart salutes/ And care of arms; and leave; and pay arrears/ Esprit de corps; and hints for young recruits'. Reviews were glittering affairs and the highlight of the social calendar was an annual grand ball in Newcastle's Assembly rooms, held every year through the 19th century from 1828: 'In all, 343 ladies and gentlemen, who included nearly the whole of the gentry of the neighbourhood', interrupted only once by an outbreak of cholera.

Service in the militia had traditionally been far less glamorous, decidedly unpopular. Limited forms of conscription in the 18th century, during the Seven Years' War (1756–63) had led to riots. One, at Hexham in 1761, ended in bloodshed with forty-odd deaths as panicky North Yorkshire militia opened fire on a hostile crowd. Fears over possible French aggression in the late 1850s had led to the raising of Rifle Volunteers – altogether more fashionable than unwilling and workaday militia but, unlike their mounted contemporaries in the Yeomanry, unwaged.

Haldane's reforms of 1908 abolished old distinctions between Rifle Volunteers and Yeomanry. The Noodles were now the Northumberland Hussar Yeomanry. These measures, though long overdue, were not entirely popular. Rates of pay came down and county gentlemen, who had been used to doing things very much their own way, suddenly found themselves altogether more accountable to the War Office. All the new Territorial units from Northumberland, Durham and North Yorkshire formed part of the newly created Northumbrian Division, commanded by General R. S. S. Baden-Powell, hero of Mafeking and founder of the Scouting Movement. Territorial divisions were intended for homeland defence though many in the ranks chose to volunteer for overseas service.

It was during this epoch, when the Queen Empress ruled nearly a quarter of the earth's inhabitants, that the Royal Military Tournament got underway, a chivalric tribute to the Spartan fighting qualities of British soldiers and sailors. Officers duelled with sabres and hacked imaginary foes, represented by melons, from horseback in a ritual dubbed 'cleaving the Turk's head'. Manly displays or martial prowess were to be lauded: 'without encouraging the display of those brutal and degrading passions, which induce a couple of vagabonds, with a dislike for work, to batter each other with their fists for a wager, till one or the other can no longer stand upright.' Tommy would be fighting a very different type of war; industrial warfare on a scale and intensity never experienced before or even imagined.

It has been said, and not without truth, that Britain fielded four armies in World War I. Firstly, the original regular army and reserves that formed the BEF in 1914 – immortalised as 'the Old Contemptibles'. Next, the Territorial battalions, followed by Kitchener's New Army Battalions and, finally, the conscript army of 1917–18. The core tactical unit throughout was the battalion (typically 750–1,000 men). This was commanded by a colonel, essentially an honorary position. Actual day-to-day command was vested in the lieutenant-colonel. As a rough rule, some 10 per cent of battalion strength was kept in reserve, left out of the battle ('LOOB'), as a core around which to rebuild if the unit was badly cut up. All too often this pragmatic prophecy came to pass.

Below lieutenant-colonel, the major was the next most senior officer. He normally commanded the 150-strong HQ Company. Then 'A', 'B', 'C' and 'D' companies were each commanded by captains, all at similar notional strength. The company was then divided into four sub-units or platoons; an HQ platoon, commanded by a lieutenant with an NCO and four privates (or 'rifleman' in a rifle unit); then four other platoons, numbered 1–4, usually led by a second lieutenant (subaltern), with four NCOs and 32 privates. The platoon itself was broken down into sections, the smallest tactical unit, each of eight men and an NCO.

Crucially, the infantry battalion in 1914 possessed only two

The **Vickers**, manufactured by Vickers-Armstrong on Tyneside, was a .303 calibre, belt-fed, water-cooled machine gun with a cyclic rate of around 500 rounds per minute. It was famed for its reliability and robustness. It required a crew of eight, a full section with one firer and one loader: the rest carried weapons, tools and ammunition.

The **Lewis** Automatic machine gun remained in service from 1914 to 1953. It was a .303 calibre, drum-fed light MG which used a 47-round box with a cyclic rate of 500 rounds per minute. At 28 lb, it was far more portable than the Vickers and had a marked effect on British infantry tactics.

Vickers medium machine guns. From 1915 firepower was significantly enhanced by the introduction of lighter automatic weapons, such as the Lewis gun. Latterly, the medium machine gunners were transferred to the Machine Gun Corps and the number of Lewis guns available was increased from four per battalion to four times that number and double that again after the Somme.

Initially, in 1914, four battalions, under a brigadier-general, formed a brigade and three brigades a division. This larger unit was commanded by a major-general and possessed its own signallers, medical staff, engineers and gunners. Three, perhaps four, divisions would be formed into an army corps, led by a lieutenant-general. A number of corps (between four and six) would constitute an army. By 1918 Britain had five armies deployed on the Western Front with a total ration strength of over a million.

Haldane's plan had been that county Territorial associations would be responsible for any large expansion in army numbers. True to their task, these immediately began to recruit when war was declared. They were, at the outset, so successful that by November 1914 not only had all shortfalls been made good but recruiting was some 25 per cent over capacity.

Kitchener had other ideas. Partly he was unconvinced by the part-time soldiers. He realised, perhaps uniquely, that the war would be both long and hard. He proposed to raise 70 new divisions to bolster the six regular and 14 Territorial. He held that the existing county system could not hope to build armed forces to compete with the Kaiser's conscripted hordes. Raising a 'New Army' from the general populace was a mammoth undertaking. The first call for six divisions went out on 7 August. He wanted 100,000 men. This call (K1) was soon followed by K2 and K3 on 11 and 13 September respectively, aimed at raising a further dozen divisions.

As a consequence the county associations found themselves competing with the War Office, though, by the end of 1914, the overall strength of the Territorials had doubled. On 15 September 1914, these 'Terriers' were called upon to volunteer for active service abroad. They would be amateurs no more. Thereafter, recruitment was in the hands of local cross-party committees. On 15 January 1915 in Durham and in other counties, men of otherwise good physique but who had been below the minimum height requirement of 5 foot 3, were recruited to 'bantam' battalions with the standard reduced to five foot. Miners tend to be stocky, and Durham miners flocked to the bantam battalions.

Tommy Atkins in 1914 was pretty much universal. He came from the old pre-war regular army and his average age was 28. Most regulars and reservists were drawn from poor, working-class backgrounds, either the industrial slums or rural shires where standards of living for most farm workers were little better. Their officers were provided, in the main, by the public school system. These two worlds had very little in common. The average subaltern (life expectancy on the Western Front – six

Field Marshal Herbert Horatio Kitchener
(1850–1916) originally came to fame after defeating the Mahdi's successor at Omdurman in 1898 – avenging Gordon and conquering the Sudan. He was Chief of Staff during the Second Boer War and then commander-in-chief in India 1902–09, where he and Lord Curzon did not get on. Forceful, autocratic and brilliant, Kitchener became Secretary of State for War and was one of the few to perceive that the war would be long and costly. He could never quite reconcile his military instincts with ministerial policy, rather cramping 'Wullie' Robertson, the Chief of the Imperial General Staff. Kitchener drowned aboard HMS *Hampshire* when she went down taking him to Russia on a top-secret mission in 1916.

WESTERN FRONT 1914 - 1918

▪▪▪▪▪▪▪▪	▬ ▬ ▬	▬▬▬▬	••••
END OF 1914	GERMAN OFFENSIVES 1918	ALLIED OFFENSIVES 1918	ARMISTICE LINE 1918

weeks) was likely to be a good 6 inches (150 mm) taller than any of the squaddies he commanded.

While 1914 saw a vast outpouring of patriotic fervour, it was not the only motivation to join up. Enlistment was a cure for unemployment, for boredom, and offered a chance to see the world. Plus it was a means of escape – many joined up to avoid life's complications, adopting aliases. For most working-class people, civilian life was grindingly hard, desperately poor, overcrowded, insanitary, and all too often short. The army offered a chance for adventure as well as travel. Few ordinary people had ventured abroad. Mainland Europe was unknown, exotic – far more remote in their eyes than the most ambitious long haul would be today.

Kitchener's new army volunteers were younger than the regulars of the BEF, many just 18. Some were underage. At Essex Farm CGWG Cemetery, just north of Ypres, lies the grave of Joseph Valentine Strudwick (he preferred Joe). He didn't quite make his 16th birthday, dying in January 1916. There are many others. Conversely, the oldest man killed was 68.

In khaki

In terms of tactics and training, lessons that could and should have been learnt from colonial wars were often overlooked. The straight shooting, adept and very tough Boers took a heavy toll during the opening stages of the Second Boer War. Lord Roberts introduced levels of training that placed far more emphasis on fire and movement. Marksmanship was prized and by 1914, Tommy could fire 12–14 rounds a minute and expect to kill his man at 600 yards (550 metres). The record set in 1913 was 38 aimed shots in a single minute.

The Germans with their heavier Mauser bolt could not match the versatility of the Lee version, which permitted the shooter to fire continuously, working the bolt without dropping the stock from his shoulder. This paid off in 1914 to the extent that the Germans, when they first encountered the BEF at Mons in August, thought they were facing men armed with automatic weapons. Tommy was better armed than his adversaries. Defeats in South Africa meant that bull, Blanco and square bashing were augmented with new more flexible drills stressing methods of attack, retreat and the full use of cover.

Such was the rush to join the colours in 1914, so overwhelming was the response to Kitchener's call, that the army's capacity to feed, house, equip and train these vast, enthusiastic hordes was overwhelmed. Officers on leave from the Indian Army, from officer training corps based in schools and universities were all dragged in. It's small wonder the lingo of the New

Army formations would resonate with words and phrases that originated on the Veldt or among the foothills of the Hindu Kush. For the recruits, their first months were often spent in makeshift camps, without uniforms, still in the Sunday 'civvies' they'd worn to sign up. They were officered in many cases by ageing retirees, whose experience was a world away from the new realities of industrial war. Undeterred, by the end of that first year, 1,190,000 volunteers had signed up.

For the first two years of the war, Britain and the Empire relied solely upon volunteers. This was unique; all the other Great Powers needed mass conscription from the outset. But the war took everything, it consumed blood and sacrifice at a rate undreamed of. Every day newspapers recorded the litany of death, page after page, column after column. Scarcely a family in the land remained untouched. Swollen by volunteers, some regiments, like the Northumberland Fusiliers would field 52 battalions, the Durham Light Infantry, 38. It still wasn't enough. Lord Derby became the architect of wartime conscription, an anathema to the British but the great flood of willing volunteers had dried to a trickle. Derby's scheme was originally limited to

Canvas webbing was of the 1908 pattern, state of the art in its day. With no restrictions across the chest it could easily be slung on and taken off. The 3-inch-wide waist-belt, fitted to a pair of narrower shoulder straps, secured five .303 ammunition pouches on each side, a bayonet hanger or frog, water bottle holder, haversack, pack, supporting straps and an entrenching tool carrier for both blade and handle. Messing kit was slung from the pack. Many of Kitchener's new army had to make do with a half-way house which comprised leather webbing, similar in design but with belt-hung ammo pouches reminiscent of earlier patterns.

unmarried males according to age. Later conscription became more universal; by April 1918 men aged over 50 were being called up. The patriotic myth had turned sour.

Tommy went to war in coarse heavy wool tunic and trousers, robust but chafing. He had a woollen issue shirt and underwear, the shirt so rough that many shaved it before use. Recruits from the industrial slums were delighted by three square meals a day. Many were under-size and underfed. The army built them up; they put on pounds and inches, good solid muscle, during training. In 1914 there were no steel helmets, and the men wore peaked caps that, while elegant, gave absolutely no protection. Their calves were encased in woollen wrappings or puttees (intended to prevent wet and dirt getting inside the boots). Wound round the leg from the boot upwards, they were tricky to get on and soon got very wet. On Tommy's feet were stout leather boots with hobnails, fearfully uncomfortable as feet swelled from forced marches on hot, unyielding paving stones.

He was also issued with a woollen greatcoat that – like his service dress – was warm and durable, rather too warm in summer and not warm enough in winter. When it got wet it stayed wet. In the trenches lice became a constant irritant. The creatures laid eggs in the seams of tunics which even boiling wouldn't kill. Jackets had to be steamed and ironed, carefully crunching the eggs. On the march back after many visits to bath houses behind the lines, where bodies and kit were scrubbed, the men would feel the old, horribly familiar itching erupt as they sweated.

Herbert Waugh from Newcastle was very much a Saturday night soldier, an aspiring professional who had joined the rather smart 6th 'City' Battalion of the Northumberland Fusiliers:

All battalions of infantry were and are very much alike. They were composed of the same type of men, who dressed alike, were armed in the same way, trained in the same way, and fought and suffered in the same places and in almost exactly the same circumstances. Throughout that August Bank Holiday weekend, there had been incredible headlines in the newspapers and then, one midnight a special postman delivered a small, blue form which intimated that the Battalion would parade in St. George's Drill Hall at six o'clock the following morning.

They were still there waiting at noon. The CSM 'whose South African Medal ribbons lent great weight to his words' was heard to prophesy, 'this is too big a thing to last, it will all; be over in three weeks': so much for the voice of experience.

Those of the 'collar and cuff' brigade enjoyed a relatively calm if somewhat tedious first winter in khaki. Their time, as days shortened, was spent digging trenches at Backworth and guard duties at Blyth, which as a thriving port, was thought to merit the Germans' hostile intent (none came). Battalion 'pub crawls' enlivened cold, dark winter days and nights spent in billets in mining hamlets. The weekend warriors discovered that the nation's martial fury had so swelled that they were no longer caricatures in uniform but heroes in khaki, even though they had yet to fire a shot in anger.

The TA was now 'guarding the shores of old England while Jack is busy on the sea'. When the call to volunteer for overseas service

Northumberland Fusiliers in captured equipment at St. Eloi. (Tasmanian Archive and Heritage Office Commons: W. L. Crowther Library)

went out, all flocked. The pressure was subtle but considerable. As the battalion paraded, officers called for all who were willing to serve abroad to 'slope arms'. Everyone did. Many a loyal toast followed in the fleshpots and ale houses of the metropolis. Then, it was back to digging trenches.

> The footsoldier is a professional dawn-watcher; he has been so since Hadrian's legionaries peered northwards from the crags at Housesteads. This is the hour of fate. There are three stages in the life of an ex-soldier: (1) the 'fed up and let's forget it' stage (2) the annual reunion stage and (3) the arm-chair and grandchildren stage.

Waugh was writing some 16 years after the end of the war. Winter was enlivened by airship raids, the dreaded Zeppelins 'a cigar-shaped shadow'. Despite much drama and standing-to, punctuated by the odd angry shot, these monsters passed overhead without incident.

'Some enthusiastic statistician has calculated the average duration of an infantry subaltern's sojourn at the front … as a matter of two or three weeks. We were untried, unbroken. We had a fresh nerve, health and youth. There was an end of term spirit about.' Hours of boring oratory from senior officers and padres were made memorable by one sermon on the eve of battle: 'Many of us who are standing here will not live to see the end of this war, and those who do will be martyrs to rheumatism before they are forty!' As the battalion marched away from their homes in north-east England they sang *It's a Long Way to Tipperary*, *Who's Your Lady Friend* and *Blaydon Races*.

When Waugh, blooded and wounded at St. Julien in the Ypres salient in 1915, finally returned from war he would be sounding an altogether more sombre note:

> Do you remember (you at the street corner or you in your private office), the thaw near Peronne which turned dry trenches into

miniature canals, the march up to Arras in the snow, when someone burst a blood vessel and died by the roadside, the promulgation of a court martial before daybreak near a Belgian farmhouse, followed by a volley in the next field and, within two hours, a newly filled grave in the field beyond?

1743	First recorded instance of British soldiers referred to as 'Tommy Atkins'.
1854–56	The Crimean War. British public begins to be aware of the need to provide for soldiers.
1857–59	Indian Mutiny.
1870s/80s	The Cardwell and Childers Reforms reorganise and reform the British Army.
1878–80	Second Afghan War.
1879	Zulu War.
1880	First Boer War.
1890	Kipling publishes 'Tommy Atkins'.
1898	Kitchener's River War, battle of Omdurman.
1899–1902	Second Boer War.
1902	Short Magazine Lee Enfield Rifle (SMLE) introduced.
1908	The Haldane Reforms; creation of the Territorial Army (TA).
1914	28 June: Archduke Franz Ferdinand and Duchess Sophie murdered in Sarajevo.
	August: Britain declares war on Germany, battles of Mons and Le Cateau. First call for divisions for Kitchener's New Army.
	September: battle of the Marne.
	October: battle of Armentières.
	October/November: first battle of Ypres.
	December: Christmas truce.
1915	Introduction of Brodie helmets.
	February: start of Gallipoli campaign.
	April: Second battle of Ypres. First use of chlorine gas by Germans at Pilckem Ridge.

	Spring/early summer: British offensives at Neuve Chapelle, Festubert and Aubers Ridge.
	June: introduction of gas hoods.
	July: National Registration Act requires all British men not in the military to register.
	September: battle of Loos.
	October: Lord Derby launches the Group Scheme.
1915–18	Sinai and Palestine campaign.
1916	January: withdrawal from Gallipoli. Military Service Act provided for the conscription of single men between 18 and 41. The scheme is extended to married men in May.
	April: surrender at Kut.
	July–November: battle of the Somme. First use of British tanks at Flers-Courcelette.
1916–18	Salonika campaign.
1917	April: battle of Arras.
	June: battle of Messines.
	July–November: third battle of Ypres.
	November: battle of Cambrai.
1918	March–July: Kaiserschlact offensives.
	April: Upper age for conscription under the Military Service Act raised to 50.
	August: battle of Amiens, 'Black Day of the German Army'.
	August–November: the Hundred Days.
	11 November: the Armistice.
1920	Unveiling of the Cenotaph.
1927	Opening of the Menin Gate.
1932	Opening of the Thiepval Memorial.

ABBREVIATIONS

BEF	British Expeditionary Force
CO	Commanding officer
CWGC	Commonwealth War Graves Commission
DLI	Durham Light Infantry
DCRO	Durham County Records Office
HE	high explosive
HQ	Headquarters
KOSB	King's Own Scottish Borderers
KOYLI	King's Own Yorkshire Light Infantry
MC	Military Cross
MG	machine gun
MGC	Machine Gun Corps
MGO	machine-gun officer
MO	medical officer
NCO	non-commissioned officer
RAMC	Royal Army Medical Corps
RAP	regimental aid post
RE	Royal Engineers
RFC	Royal Flying Corps
RNF	Royal Northumberland Fusiliers (though the 'Royal' was awarded after 1918)

UNIFORMS AND KIT

British marching kit P08 of 1914, showing large pack and entrenching tool holder. (Rob and Emily Horne)

Side view of P08 webbing showing frog, bayonet and entrenching tool shaft. (Emily Horne)

The clumsy gas hood, ill fitting, constrictive and prone to misting. (Emily Horne)

Typical 'Tommy' marching kit from 1916. He wears the steel Brodie pattern helmet, P08 webbing, gas mask and case with the .303 SMLE rifle with 10-round box magazine, the best rifle of the war, latterly used by Taliban fighters against British troops in Afghanistan in the 21st century. (Emily Horne)

German infantry 1914 marching kit. Note the leather webbing, Mauser K98 bolt action rifle and the distinctive if impractical pickelhaube.
(Emily Horne)

Later German kit; much of the pre-war uniform detail has gone, he now wears the steel helmet and carries a stick grenade.
(Emily Horne)

CHAPTER 1

DEADLOCK

1914

Then I knew that I'd been sleeping, while the Yeomen were awake;
I had simply been 'a slacker' when my country was at stake.
So I joined the gay Commercials, and I did the Swedish drill,
Till I found myself expanding and my chest began to fill;
And when marching with my comrades in the scarlet shoulder-straps,
I could see another meaning in the blue around the caps.

O. Hall, *And the Blue Around their Caps*

From Mons to the Aisne

IN THE EARLY DAYS OF THE WAR, General Sir John French led 100,000 men of the BEF, divided into two corps, each with two divisions. Sir Douglas Haig commanded I Corps. Dour and uncommunicative, the prudish Scot was scandalised by French's numerous affairs.

One of those who marched up the dusty pave to Mons was J. B. W. Pennyman, from Ormesby Hall near Middlesbrough. He served as MGO in 2nd Battalion, KOSB, from the start of hostilities until he was wounded on the Aisne in October 1914. The battalion embarked from Dublin on 13 August 1914:

Left Dublin on the Bibby Liner 'Gloucestershire' – expecting a hostile demonstration from the citizens but none occurred. 14th August: We passed quite close to the Cornish coast. I'm sure there was a general though not expressed idea that for each man this might be his last sight of England. We were packed very tight and the ship and each regiment messed in the saloon. At Havre, teams of London dockers were already in situ.

17th August: Left camp at 04.00 hours, entrained at 06.00. We all, officers and men, performed our ablutions and shaved at the station. Breakfast was at 07.00 hours and we left two hours later, still having no idea of our destination. We were in a passenger train and reasonably comfortable, arriving at Rouen about midday. We were cheered by the French who were begging souvenirs; half the men gave away their badges. Everyman we saw in the fields first pretended to twist his moustache up to his eyes and then to cut his throat to show by what means the Kaiser should die! About 22.00 or 23.00 hours we passed through Amiens.

22nd August: We crossed into Belgium today. The inhabitants had heard we were starving and all classes loaded us with fruit (mostly unripe), cigarettes, tobacco, matches and wine. It was an awful job getting the battalion along through these towns and I shall never forget it … we might have been marching through the slums of Glasgow, except for the language of the people. At about 17.00 hours we arrived at the Mons-Conde Canal, where we took up our posts for the night. I put my guns in a little sandbag fort which I built on the lock abutment with the guns trained straight down the canal.

23rd August: We were not attacked early on so I looked around for a better location for my guns. A line of houses stood on the opposite side of the canal and it seemed the only place I could get any field of fire would be from the second floor of the highest house. I knew we should have to leave on the arrival of the first shell. The section hacked loopholes through the walls and piled sandbags so the guns could fully cover the lock and its approaches. By late morning things were beginning to hot up.

A, B & C companies were lining the meadows in front facing half-right. We could see the Boche deploying around 900 yards

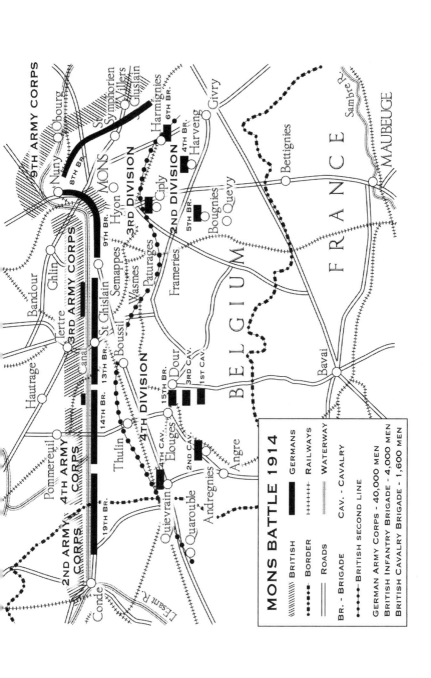

MONS BATTLE 1914

BRITISH	GERMANS
BORDER	RAILWAYS
ROADS	WATERWAY

BR. - BRIGADE   CAV. - CAVALRY

●●●● BRITISH SECOND LINE

GERMAN ARMY CORPS - 40,000 MEN
BRITISH INFANTRY BRIGADE - 4,000 MEN
BRITISH CAVALRY BRIGADE - 1,600 MEN

in front. They were beginning to filter into woods across the canal in front of our position and were engaged by A & C companies. A group of Boche, possibly an MG section, were spotted in front and we laid out four of them with our first traverse. We then took on any Germans we saw in the open and did considerable damage. This was our first experience of killing people. It was rather horrible but satisfying.

Our infantry were heavily engaged and taking casualties. D company was attempting to winkle the Germans out of the wood. Suddenly I saw the front edge of the wood lined with Germans and surmised that they were going to try and rush D company, so I concentrated the full fire from both guns on the fringes of the wood and the Germans retreated. Their eyrie was now a prime target: Gilmartin asked me whether our sandbags were bullet proof and, as he spoke; one bullet just came through and dropped on the floor. It was really red hot. Soon the fire on us became so hot indeed that bullets started coming through the walls.

… I went along the line seeking a good fire position; shells were by now pounding the houses. The colonel was walking calmly up and down sucking on his old pipe and not caring a damn. By 18.00 hours we had orders to withdraw, on orderly retirement covered by the YLI. The swarm of refugees tumbling back included our hosts of the night before from the lock-keepers house. This was now blown to pieces. With his Gallic allies on his right pulling back, French ordered a retreat.

As the division retreated, back the long weary miles over which they'd earlier advanced, they drew on towards Le Cateau. It was harvest time. Heat lay heavy as a thick blanket, caking men and animals in mingled sweat and dust. Le Cateau was in fact a larger battle than Mons. General Horace Smith-Dorrien, commander of II Corps, wished to deliver what he termed 'a stopping blow' to halt the Germans and allow his corps to fall back unmolested. Although the BEF saw off a number of German attacks and then continued its withdrawal in good order, the day was dearly bought: some 7,812 men and 38 guns were lost.

26th August: At 16.30 hours we relieved another regiment in some trenches … well dug and well-sited, but only very short, holding a platoon at most, and very far apart. About dawn the CO and adjutant galloped round the trenches, said we had to stay on and not retire under any circumstances. I had an excellent field of fire, about 800 yards and we thought we would do some damage before we were all put out of action.

To their right front stood Le Cateau church and a crossroads. The poplar-lined Cateau–Cambrai road ran before them. 'At about 19.00 hours we saw enormous masses of German infantry deploying around three miles ahead and realised we were in for a big thing. There was much heavy shelling but little damage, the Boche advanced to within around 2,000 yards. Troops to our front, being without orders began to retire but the colonel just stood there on his great horse till they were all back in their trenches and then he trotted back. By some miracle he wasn't hit.' As darkness began to fall, Pennyman rounded up a platoon-sized group of stragglers and marched on:

We lined a potato field and prepared to give any German Uhlans a warm reception. None came and we were relieved by our own cavalry. The battalion had suffered casualties and men captured. The Colonel was wounded and captured in the retreat. I was knocked flat by a shell, though seemingly unhurt. A few days afterward, however, my attention was called to a neat little bullet hole in my Glengarry strings: A very near miss indeed.

27th August: Our retreat continued, the men were very tired. I noticed some horrible looking carcases in the mud by the roadside. They looked so dirty and beastly that nobody had touched them but, on closer examination, I found them to be perfectly good British ration meat. So we hacked some flesh off and went on till we saw a chance of cooking them.

By the village of Beaurevoir the KOSBs harvested potatoes growing in the fields and later cooked a grand stew in a vast witches' cauldron that an old lady kindly provided for the task.

'All said this was the best meal they'd had since leaving Dublin!'

> 28th August: The RV was now to be at Noyon, another 20 miles away; lots of stragglers were coming in, some marching, a lucky few in motor lorries. In that week we'd marched over a hundred miles, fought three battles and two scraps [skirmishes].

Next day, 29 August passed as a much-needed rest, followed by a moonlit march in the cool of night. More hard marches followed between 29 August and 1 September and the state of the men's feet giving rise to worry. On 1 September it was another rearguard action, 'the enemy had no artillery or else it was very soon put out of action, and we gather what little artillery we had with us did tremendous execution amongst the enemy's infantry. After about two hours firing we had apparently got the better of the Germans in front of us and it was rather annoying to have to retire.'

Though the Schlieffen Plan appeared to be working, there were serious cracks. Von Moltke's timidity and the rising crisis on the Eastern Front led to a thinning of the concept. Now the BEF were swinging west of Paris; 'we were hoping for a siege, at least we'd get a rest!' By 4 September they had reached Coulommes, 'ate apples, drank cider, had a rest day and moved off at 23.00 hours, passed the field of Crecy.' 6th September: 'Our retreat was at an end, we marched back to Villeneuve, some Germans appeared in the early hours but they were falling back now and we captured some Uhlan stragglers.'

The next day they 'marched to Boissy ... saw a strange RAMC major having dinner with us and thought we had a new doctor [the battalion MO had been wounded in the retreat] then we found out he had been put under arrest for stopping on the line of march to buy something!' 8 September: 'We engaged the German rearguard north-east of Doue. We were faced by German horse artillery and two cavalry regiments plus one heavy gun. The KOSB were ¾ mile in front of the British gun line and the Boche gun was plumping very large HE shells all amongst the battalion. Miraculously we sustained no casualties.'

Despite this intense weight of fire the order for the infantry to advance came through: 'We had to cross the brow of a hill – about five hundred yards of perfectly open ground of which they already had the range to a tee. The battalion doubled across this in two lines, went down through a thick wood and reformed in a railway cutting at the bottom. Nothing could have bettered the German artillery's efforts and I'm sure they thought they'd wiped us out. As a matter of fact we had twelve casualties, killed and wounded. When we got through the wood we saw the River Marne in front of us.'

Thursday 10 September, the pursuit continued: 'We marched all day through unsavoury German remains.… 11 September: I was in charge of a small group of German POWs. They were extraordinarily docile and well-behaved … all the prisoners I saw were decent looking young men, quite good class and well-nourished. Their equipment and uniforms were excellent. I saw no sign of any atrocities nor heard of any though of course these were widely reported.'

Within two days the KOSB were approaching the River Aisne. Here, the fluid front would harden as the Germans dug in along the favourable high ground beyond the river. As the borderers approached the village of Sermoise, they were held up by plunging, long-range fire. Only at dusk did they move forward into the village; 'people were very plucky gave us coffee and anything they had to eat. Our orders were to get to the river – this proved difficult in the late summer dark, the only bridge was under fire. The battalion was very tired we'd had only an hour's sleep in the last twenty-four. In the confused night the MG section got lost and we ended up back in the village where the West Kents doctor told us we could now get over the bridge.'

After a confused and difficult night Pennyman and his MG section made for the bridge at first light. The river was no more than 50 yards across, the bridge had been blown; 'the RE had made a raft but it had a very nasty habit of sinking, and when we got there we found three drowned men ... oddly the Boche were not contending the crossing.' Once over, the borderers faced a difficult task. 'The village of Missy was about ½ mile ahead, the riverbank was thickly wooded, a belt of trees thirty yards wide sloping down to the water's edge. Beyond say ½ mile of parkland rising to wooded hills full of Boche.' The West Kents were just ahead of the wood; 'but we couldn't advance and retreating meant swimming for it. By 08.00 hours the battalion was fully across and deployed in the trees. The Boche advanced into the copse some 700 yards ahead but our MG fire sent them running back as quick as they could.'

Enemy fire soon intensified. The Germans were trying to infiltrate the woods and a single platoon was detailed to occupy the ground. Murderous small-arms fire forced them back:

> the river was alive with bullets. We lost a good many men. I wanted either to advance or retire but the West Kents colonel ordered us to hold on. We swept the enemy ground with MG fire. One gun jammed, the first time this had happened. There was so much noise, verbal communication was almost impossible. A bullet went into the ground very close to me as I was working the other gun. I thought it might be a sniper who had caught sight of me so I moved three or four yards to our right. Next thing I remember was a sensation like a blow from a cricket ball in the chest. It knocked me clean down and I remember shouting as I fell and bleeding profusely at the mouth.
>
> I felt quite certain I was a 'gonner' but managed to get up and give some directions to the gunner; then I flopped down again. I passed out. I was wounded at about 14.00 hours but couldn't be got back till 19.00 and came to as I was being treated. I began to have a feeling of terrible cramp all over my chest and difficulty breathing. I was told my only chance was to lie perfectly still and flat and a healthy dose of morphine helped me to do this. Evacuation was difficult and protracted: we travelled in spring-less lorries to the railhead at Ouichy.... Later our stretchers were put into the familiar carriages 'Hommes 40; Chevaux 8'. Spring hooks

had been fitted to hold stretchers … a stretcher is a very cold, hard thing to lie on for the best part of a week.

Along the Aisne there was stalemate and the lines began to harden. The war of manoeuvre was very nearly over.

It was early in October that the BEF advanced northwards. Sir John French hoped he would be able to strike a blow against the Germans' exposed flank. He had already been reinforced by a further division to make good his earlier casualties. Encouraged by General Ferdinand Foch, Sir John believed the hinge of his successful blow would be the Belgian city of Ypres. At this point, the German high command entertained similar hopes. As the British felt their way towards Menin, they collided with large enemy forces. Flanders was about to become a major battlefield.

The first battle of Ypres

I want to tell you now sir
Before it's all forgot
That we were up at Wipers
And found it very hot

Plum & Apple (September 1915)

On 5 October 1914, the Northumberland Hussars sailed on the *Minneapolis* from Southampton for an uneventful night passage to Zeebrugge. 'The morrow broke cold and wet as we steamed slowly into harbour … It was late in the afternoon before we set off down a long typical Belgian road toward Bruges. Our reception … was ecstatic. At every hamlet along that poplar-lined stretch of pave the inhabitants would raise a cheer for "les Anglais" while little urchins would clamour for buttons & badges … pretty girls would almost drag us from our saddles to kiss us and to shake our hands.'

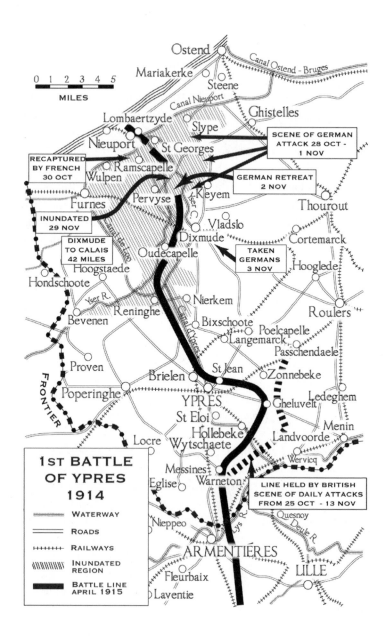

Ostend

Mariakerke

Canal Ostend - Bruges

Steene

Ghistelles

Canal Nieuport

Lombaertzyde

Slype

SCENE OF GERMAN
ATTACK 28 OCT -
1 NOV

Nieuport

St Georges

RECAPTURED
BY FRENCH
30 OCT

Ramscapelle

Wulpen

Pervyse

Kleyem

GERMAN RETREAT
2 NOV

Furnes

INUNDATED
29 NOV

Vladslo

Thourout

DIXMUDE
TO CALAIS
42 MILES

Canal de Loo

Dixmude

Cortemarck

Oudecapelle

TAKEN
GERMANS
3 NOV

Hoogstaede

Hooglede

Hondschoote

Yser R.

Nierkem

Canal d'Yser

Roulers

Reninghe

Bixschoote

Bevenen

Poelcapelle

Langemarck

Passchendaele

Proven

Brielen

St Jean

Zonnebeke

Poperinghe

YPRES

Gheluvelt

Ledeghem

St Eloi

Menin

Hollebeke

Landvoorde

Locre

Wytschaete

Wervicq

FRONTIER

Messines

Eglise

Warneton

LINE HELD BY BRITISH
SCENE OF DAILY ATTACKS
FROM 25 OCT - 13 NOV

Quesnoy

Nieppeo

Lys R.

Deule R.

1ST BATTLE
OF YPRES
1914

ARMENTIÉRES

LILLE

Fleurbaix

Laventie

=========== WATERWAY

———— ROADS

++++++++ RAILWAYS

/////////// INUNDATED
REGION

▬▬▬▬ BATTLE LINE
APRIL 1915

0 1 2 3 4 5

MILES

Captain Grant, who narrates the experience of the Noodles during the first battle of Ypres, had previously served in South Africa. The Hussars were the first Territorial unit to be shipped out. By 08.00 on 8 October the yeomanry were in the saddle, riding as the eyes and ears of 7th Division. They hoped to fight Uhlans 'but to our disappointment encountered none. Instead we discovered how unsuitable pave roads are for cavalry, and that mounted men do only less foot-slogging than infantry when a division is moving *en masse*.'

Ostend proved less congenial. The streets were chaotic as stunned refugees struggled to get clear, 'fearsome rumours as to the fate of Antwerp flew from mouth to mouth … at this period of our soldiering we were credulous and drank them in'. It was now they realised that their task was not to assist the Belgian Army as much as to cover its withdrawal, 'to shield that heroic remnant from annihilation'. They entrained for Ghent where their earlier rapturous welcome was replayed. The Noodles deployed on outpost duty and, for the first time, came under enemy fire, happily ineffectual:

> I was picturing to myself Saturday night at home, and thinking how little the boys there were dreaming of what we were doing that night, when suddenly a succession of reports sounded in the air. I must confess I could not determine whether they were rifle shots or not. Just then a shadow loomed up before me, and with an effort I spluttered out 'Halt! Who goes there?' I had my finger on the trigger and was ready for him. I felt, I must confess, much relieved when immediately there came the whispered assurance 'friend'. It was an infantryman, like myself, on outpost duty, and he enquired if I had heard anything lately. 'Yes' I replied 'I think it must have been the rumbling of transport wagons on the cobbled road.' 'No, mate' was his rejoinder, 'it was 15 rounds rapid.' The battle was drawing nearer.

Ghent was being prepared for defence. The ominous sound of explosions, signifying the destruction of bridges, barricades and barbed-wire entanglements, spread. The British were about to retreat. This time their passage would not be marked by rejoicing: '12th October; we slipped by silently and almost guiltily, the infantry with fixed bayonets, battalion after battalion, gliding past like phantoms … ourselves as rearguard. The march was rendered all the slower by a battalion of exhausted French marines and the struggling masses of refugees who congested the roads, flying from the invader with what household effects they could save, piled on their small, dog-drawn carts, accompanied in almost every case by weeping children.'

To spare their horses, the cavalry were obliged to dismount and experience the chore of marching, hard enough for infantry 'to a cavalryman, even a veteran it is worse. Not only does he have to do his share of the marching, but there is his horse to be cared for, to be fed and watered before he can attend to his own wants and then we were not veterans. The outbreak of the war had found us civilians, many in sedentary employments, and two months of strenuous training, even when accompanied by the best will in the world, can only do something toward case-hardening.'

Cavalry of the British Indian Army on the Western Front, 1914. (National Library of Scotland, via Wikimedia Commons)

Private Chrystal, a noted Geordie marksman and later sniper, was astonished to learn that a squadron of French horsemen, cuirassiers, were in fact allies. 'Whey,' he exclaimed, 'I thought them b******s wor German hoolans [Uhlans = lancers] an' I fired at the likes o' them aal day yesterday'. On 14 October the hussars clattered into the streets of Ypres 'which the enemy had looted but which had remained untouched by shells. The following day found us early on patrol. It was during one of these patrols that Sergeant-Major Hannington brought down a Uhlan with his rifle. First blood to the regiment!'

German troops were now massing in front of the British line, which was taking shape around the 'rim' of the saucer that was the Ypres Salient. The defenders' trenches snaked from Messines in the south, across the Menin Road at Gheluvelt, north to Zonnebeke and St. Julien. The westwards hinge was fixed at Langemarck and the shallow Pilckem Ridge. The attacking divisions were screened by cavalry and there were frequent jousts with probing patrols of Uhlans as the Tommies dug in. By 16 October the front had hardened. The battle would unfold as the Germans tried to dislodge the BEF from higher ground, back towards Ypres and then clear through to the Channel coast.

More aggressive patrolling followed. British tactical aims centred upon wresting control of Menin, even though the strength of the enemy presence was daily increasing. There was still some fluidity in the war. The Noodles and other cavalry units were actively engaged in an attack on 19 October. Menin proved a stage too far and intense shellfire compelled withdrawal.

Here took place a peculiar incident. A white-haired old man suddenly made a dash from one of the houses occupied by the enemy and, running with extraordinary agility across the field of fire reached our lines safely. He told us of the endless columns of 'field-greys' advancing to the attack and determined to force a passage to the Channel ports. By this time infantry and a battery of horse-artillery had come to our assistance ... this was our baptism of fire as a regiment. Of many memories of that first engagement, one of the most vivid is of a company of infantry [from 2nd Battalion, Queen's Regiment] rising from the miry field where they had been lying, advancing in perfect extended order, led by an officer with a stick, and then being mown down almost to a man by withering fire.

This doomed attempt to take Menin signalled the end of mobile warfare. With overwhelming numbers the Germans tightened the ring around Ypres and sought to squeeze out the BEF. The race was over. It was now a fight for bare survival. 'The armies were at grips. Aeroplane reconnaissance now took the place of cavalry and revealed the fact that enemy reinforcements were arriving in vast numbers behind a screen of cyclists and the ubiquitous Uhlans. In the face of overwhelming numbers, and in view of the weakness of our infantry, our role as cavalry ended about this time. It was no longer possible to push forward cavalry patrols beyond the line of infantry, especially as the latter were now pinned down to the defensive and needed an unrestricted field of fire.'

The Noodles were cavalry no more. 'From this time our role was to be a general reserve for the sorely tried infantry, to be ready at any moment to dash up and fling ourselves into any gap that appeared dangerous. It was not a pleasant task, involving, as it did, many weary hours of waiting under shellfire. Frequently we would receive orders to fill a gap some miles away, but would find on arrival that it was already filled. Nothing can be more trying than prolonged waiting under arms.'

On 22 October, with the crisis of the battle drawing near, the Hussars were roused from their weary billets in filthy dark with rain in torrents and no lights allowed. 'Hooge Chateau was our destination. We stood-to for the remainder of the night, and in the morning were ordered right forward to the trenches; here we made the acquaintance of "Black Marias" [German shells] for the first time. They would come over in groups of four and burst with a villainous roar and clouds of yellow smoke, most unpleasant to meet as we ran, as best we could in our heavy equipment, across a sodden turnip field to the assistance of the infantry.'

The footsloggers had been having a very rough time indeed. 'We found them in position in the garden of a chateau, and were immediately told to prepare it for attack. The coolness of the infantry was admirable. They had been under constant fire for several days, were ragged, unkempt and grimy, short of rations and ammunition; but not a man appeared to be weary of the fight. Above the appalling din could be heard the clear, concise orders of the officers, no less ragged than their men, but undaunted and equal to any emergency.' After a day's fighting the Noodles were withdrawn to Hooge Chateau, filthy, exhausted 'but with a feeling of mild elation at having been "blooded," at having proved ourselves equal to the occasion – a feeling akin to that of the anxious cricketer who has successfully broken his duck's egg.'

Fate would deny them any rest. No sooner had they laid aside their arms than they were needed. Once again the Noodles mounted and rode towards Klein-Zillebeke where another break-in threatened. 'Trenches were begun, roads barricaded, and houses – by this time deserted – were prepared for defence. Just as it seemed we were to be at work all night, we were relieved.' It was back to Hooge but 'on entering the grounds we were greeted by a burst of shrapnel right at the head of the column. This caused a momentary stampede among the horses … luckily there were no casualties.'

German pressure was beginning to tell. The embattled line was showing signs of imminent rupture:

> Under increasing pressure the infantry had been forced to give ground, and it was just at that moment when the gap was ominously widening that the regiment, waiting in reserve, was called on to assist. There was a hurried rush across the miry fields, and through a wood filled with dead and wounded, to the trenches where the remnants of several regiments were collected. Here we remained for several hours under very heavy rifle and shell fire, unable to retaliate very effectively, owing to the poorness of the field of fire. But these gallant riflemen stuck to it, their crisp, sharp fire orders never seeming to falter. Then came the crowning incident of the day. A

Wounded at side of the road at the battle of Menin Road. (Frank Hurley, State Library of New South Wales, via Wikimedia Commons)

line of Scots Guards suddenly rose to the order 'Come on, the Scots Guards!' echoed by Major Sidney's 'Come on, Northumberland Hussars!' and together Guards and Hussars charged against a swaying mass of grey figures and finally drove them over the hill.

On 24 October, arguably the most serious crisis developed as 2nd Battalion, Royal Warwickshires, were inexorably pushed back, allowing the enemy to infiltrate Polygon Wood, which the Noodles had so stoutly defended the day before. Once again the cavalry, mounted infantry now, cantered up the shell-scarred line of the Menin Road, arrow straight from Ypres. 'A hurried gallop … and an advance in open order across the usual sticky turnip field brought us to the forefront of the battle. Too far in fact, for raking fire from a machine gun played havoc in the ranks, and was responsible for most of the casualties – Major Sidney, Captain Kennard and Lieutenant Clayton, amongst others being wounded while several men were killed. Soon, the yeomanry were lying down and maintaining a steady fire. There was no reserve. Each did the work of ten.'

The scarred wood wasn't lost, though it was a close-run thing. By mid-morning, British counter-attacks, supported by French cavalry, threw the Germans just about out. 'A battalion of Welsh Fusiliers now advanced to reinforce the line, a battalion no more than three hundred strong and officered by the Colonel, adjutant and three subalterns, of whom two were barely 'off-parade' [i.e. newly commissioned]. At this period of the battle such a battalion was relatively strong [so terrible the rate of attrition] … In the early afternoon the enemy attacked the junction of the 20th and 21st Infantry Brigades just east of Gheluvelt, and again the position seemed desperate.'

This time it was the Grenadier Guards who charged and won the day though, like every respite in the salient, casualties were high. 'We were relieved and returned to Hooge, not a few horses, alas, with empty saddles … our troubles were not over, however, for we were shelled all night and sleep was well nigh impossible.' For the Noodles a day of much-needed rest followed the fighting for Polygon Wood. Along the line, pressure never slackened. 'The odds against us we learned were at least eight to one with no reserves to fall back on. Some idea of the desperate nature of the fighting may be gathered from the fact that the Welsh regiment with whom we had been associated the previous day, were now reduced to fifty men with no officers. But here the marvellous discipline of the regular army asserted itself and those magnificent men fought under the command of a lance-corporal.'

For two days, there was a brief respite as both sides drew breath, 'the artillery fire of the Germans, though still unpleasantly persistent, was rather less intense and pointed to a reorganisation of the enemy for further attacks.' This was ominous, the lull before the storm. Some good news was to be had, the BEF's 1st Division had accomplished prodigious slaughter by Langemarck, 'piles of German dead and captured'. Cynicism would soon creep into Tommy's reading of the daily news but not yet; 'at that time we greedily swallowed such stories without the customary grain of salt, and perhaps it was as well that we did so.'

On 29 October, the storm over the salient burst once more, 'the fight continuing with the greatest intensity for six days, perhaps the six most critical days of the war'. The line to the east rested on an axis Gheluvelt–Zanvoorde; 21 Brigade had the right and 20 Brigade the left with 22nd in reserve. The next German wave struck the vulnerable hinge between 1st Division and 20 Brigade. The Guards were forced to give ground till desperate counter-attacks succeeded in winning it back. Pressure then swelled on the right where the vital crossroads junction on the ridge was taken. The Noodles 'cooperated in the counter-attack on the left and was heavily engaged all day. At nightfall our line, though slightly pressed back, still included Gheluvelt and Zanvoorde. The attacks of the enemy were renewed on the 30th, and overwhelming numbers and superiority of artillery fire had their inevitable result. The cavalry on our right were forced to withdraw, thereby exposing our flank, and a murderous enfilade fire from field-batteries annihilated the Royal Welsh Fusiliers, who died practically to a man.'

Raw courage could not ultimately contest this incessant storm of German steel. Sustained attacks down the Menin Road bludgeoned a breach into Gheluvelt. Overall, it appeared as though the battle was now lost: 'transport came hurrying down the road in confusion; the heavier guns, at this time mainly 4.7's [shells] were being hurriedly withdrawn. Field batteries were hastily limbered up by exhausted gunners and galloped across fields, and as hastily unlimbered and wheeled around into action again. Here was a scene of indescribable confusion and dismay, heightened by the pitiable stream of wounded men who plodded painfully to the rear, unbroken, however, in spirit, as their shouts of "give them hell, boys" showed.'

It seemed the line could not possibly hold, as thin and taut as a drum string, with the wailing crescendo of German shells pounding like a demonic curse. The 20th Brigade, dreadfully thinned, nearer a battalion at best, struggled forward and again restored the line. As the enemy faltered, the British 'performed prodigious feats of valour with the bayonet, attacking time after time with incomparable spirit, finally driving an enemy at least six times their strength headlong before them into the night'. For the moment at least, the Germans had had enough. Although 1 November was a relatively quiet day, the following day, the British learnt that Kaiser Wilhelm was to tour the German positions and add fresh heart to their faltering offensive.

'Once again, under the fiercest attacks the 1st Division was obliged to give ground … all available reserves failed to stem the enemy advance'. This final time it seemed as though weight of numbers must win through, 'once again the regiment was hurried forward into immediate reserve. The shelling was very heavy, heavier perhaps than ever before. But the 7th Division held firm, and attack after attack was hurled back without appreciable loss of ground.'

Like a spring tide, successive breakers of German attacks threatened to sweep aside the thinned and exhausted lines but Tommy, bloodied, battered, begrimed and exhausted, somehow held. To all intents the battle was virtually over and the BEF had come through. The price had been high.

Winter

After the cauldron of Ypres, the Noodles were rotated out of the line and rested for two weeks, a generous furlough by later standards: 'The enemy had been driven from Meteren but a few weeks before, the inhabitants told us; a German, in fact, had been killed nearby. But the place, like Bailleul, had hardly suffered, though it had been stripped of course, of the necessities of life, so much so that "*les Allemands ont tout, tout, tout pris*"'.

At last the mounted infantry were issued with bayonets and there was some patrolling towards Ploegsteert. Fresh attacks were being launched against the salient though the battle was rapidly running out of steam. Winter was approaching; 'the weather about this time took a change for the worse. Days of incessant rain were followed by snow and sleet – Flanders at its worst. How bad that can be only a seasoned campaigner knows.'

The regiment moved again, this time finding themselves stuck between Armentières and Laventie. It was not a region likely to commend itself to the Northumbrians, more used to the rugged topography of their native shore: 'The ground is absolutely flat, unspeakably dreary and featureless. The soil is heavy clay and under the lightest rain becomes a morass. It seems to rain most days in winter, and there is often a mist of deadly coldness. To strike water even in summer it is seldom necessary to dig more than a few feet; in winter it lies on the surface.'

Nor was this bleak picture enlivened by the inhabitants. 'In these farms dwelt farmers of prodigious age, who tilled the ground in the absence of the young men, and some emaciated stock.' The war was in its relative infancy, the Western Front had yet to sink into the routine of trenches, month in, month out, regardless of season. That vast hinterland of supply which would spread out behind the lines into a network of biblical proportions did not exist. 'At this early stage no flaring announcement of English beer met the eye of the tired warrior trudging from the trench to his comfortless barn. Any luxuries beyond the bare rations were hard to come by, except in parcels from home. There were no canteens, hence a perpetual shortage of tobacco and cigarettes and of most extras that make life worth living even in war. There were no Divisional concert parties, no cinemas and, at first, no baths.'

As the Noodles were in general reserve, their duties were varied but universally unedifying, the minutiae of war. After the dash and drama of Ypres, they guarded bridges and crossroads, practised the perfect management of horse-lines. 'The orderly room staffs discovered that a war of attrition means an endless war of forms and paper, and were probably busier than anyone else. Meanwhile rumours of spies again revived. Patrols were everywhere on the alert, and were ordered to acquaint themselves with the physiognomy of every inhabitant …'

This was not an idle fear as Nurse Katherine Luard recorded in her diary:

> Saturday, November 28th 1914. – A sergeant of the 10th Hussars told me he was in a house with some supposed Belgian refugees. He noticed that when a little bell near the ceiling rang one of them always dashed upstairs. He put a man upstairs to trace this bell and intercept the Belgian. It was connected with the little trap-door of a pigeon-house. When a pigeon came in with a message, this door rang the bell and they went up and got the message. They didn't reckon on having British in the house. They were shot next morning.

For the yeomanry their brief war of movement was over. As the year drew to a close 'Christmas came and went, with its football matches and the informal armistice of the trenches; but in a few days the guns were barking as merrily as ever'. From now on they would live and fight from the trenches. As water was seldom more than 2 or 3 feet below the surface, even in comparatively dry seasons, the trenches were in most places a compromise:

'A narrow, shallow ditch supplied the trench proper, above it to front and back were piled sandbags, usually in higgledy-piggledy manner … even if they were well laid the Boche gunner could be trusted to see that they did not long remain so. Rough traverses there were, very necessary when the Boche sniper commanded the flanks with enfilade fire.' Beyond the parapet lay the wire, still in thin belts at this early stage 'and continually preyed on by enemy trench mortars and shells'. Life within was far from agreeable: 'Before the days of revetting wire and frames, of iron and timber, even of duckboards, the painfully constructed trench was at the mercy of the weather. A heavy shower even in the heat of summer would reduce the interior to a quagmire. In the height of winter, conditions were unspeakable. An endless winding ditch, filled with glutinous mud of extraordinary tenacity, led past the support trench to the firing line proper – a rather wide, deeper ditch and consequently with the greater depth of water, not infrequently waist high. There the infantry would pass their tour of duty, harassed by enemy snipers, who seemed inevitably to command the weakest points of the system, and to a shell-fire to which their own batteries, for very lack of ammunition, were unable to respond.'

This was no life for a cavalryman.

CHAPTER 2

STALEMATE

1915

IF YOU TRAVEL TO YPRES TODAY, you will find a beautiful Flemish city of fine avenues, dominated by the grand and lofty bulk of the cloth hall, steep, red-tiled gables, surrounded by a mighty ring of Vauban walls, designed in the late 17th century with a view to keeping the English out. If you were unaware of the history of the place you could easily be forgiven for thinking the town largely unchanged over several centuries. In fact all that you behold is rebuilt, stone upon precious stone. So thorough, so unrelenting, so massive was the destruction wrought by German shells that the whole was virtually obliterated. Churchill wanted the shattered wreck left in 1918 as a fossilised memorial. The locals disagreed. Before the autumn of 1914, few in Britain had heard of the place. The names of nearly 55,000 British and Commonwealth dead, graves unknown, carved lovingly into the sepulchre of the Menin Gate, offer eloquent and silent testimony.

The Salient

Imagine a saucer and the city of Ypres in the depression, around a thin, barely noticeable ring of higher ground to the east and

Field Marshal Lord Plumer at the unveiling of the Menin Gate memorial, 1927. (University of Victoria Libraries, Canada, via Wikimeadia Commons)

south, like a gentle rim. That is the Ypres salient. He who holds the rim dominates the saucer. By 1915, it was the Germans. The British position was horribly exposed. Wet, low-lying Flanders ('Flooded Land') proved an uncomfortable and ungracious host. By the end of the first battle of Ypres, the Germans held not just the high ground to the east, ending in the village of Passchendaele, but also Hill 60, two miles southwest of the ruined city and the Wytschaete–Messines ridge further south.

Most historians date trench warfare proper from September 1915 as the retreating Germans began to dig in along the Chemin des Dames Ridge. From that point on the line swiftly began to solidify, from the North Sea to the Swiss border – 475 miles. By the end of 1915 estimates suggested each mile of front was amplified twenty times by the maze of trenches behind it. As the war ground on the scale increased. By 1918 the whole troglodyte network extended for some 25,000 miles.

Digging in the heavy ground of Flanders got no deeper than a couple of feet before encountering the water table. Unable to dig, Tommy built a system of sandbag redoubts. The Germans referred to these as box trenches, their white zigzag scars running across the wet plain, a comfortingly easy target for their gunners. Their artillery would batter what was left of the carefully wrought system of water defences that held the hungry sea at bay, ratcheting up the misery quotient.

Where ground permitted, the trench would be dug down some 8 feet, and would be about 12 wide. A shelf or firestep was built in to the forward-facing flank to form a fighting platform. Sandbags were used to form a parapet and, to the rear, a parados. The former was generally lower than the former so defenders' profiles would be broken up and thus less exposed to snipers. Distances between the opposing lines could be half a mile or only a matter of yards.

George Hilton, 2nd Battalion, KOSB, was born in 1872 and served in the ranks for eight years before being commissioned in 1900 as a second lieutenant in DCLI. He then joined KOSB as lieutenant in 1905 and by December 1916 was a major. At 43, Hilton was a relatively old man. Very much a career soldier, he was sent out at the turn of the year. '3 January: the enemy was about 22 yards distant and during the time we were changing threw up flares by means of pistols, these burn very brightly and the men had to crouch until the light burned down … we were sniped a very little during the night.'

The trench sides, even in firm dry chalk upland, would not stand without support. Timber and corrugated iron had to be brought in and fatigue parties kept busy hour after exhausting hour, maintaining the structure. '5 January: The dugouts are in a field north of a farm. It is a very large farm and a pity to see it in this condition. There is a petrol engine here just installed and it looks like being ruined … lots of tobacco out hanging up, of course it will be ruined too.' '9 January: We marched to the trenches and I took over a trench on the left of the road. It was a perfect maze of trenches and very difficult to understand. Fryer and myself went to shelled out Smelly Pig Farm and got some straw and tried to make things comfortable.'

A trench was never a purely linear feature. If it were, once penetrated, the enemy, gaining a foothold, could rake the entire length. Instead, they were built as an alternating system of projecting fire-bays linked by traverses. To attack such a trench meant 'bombing up the traverses'. An attacking section would be divided between bombers, grenade throwers and bayonet men. The former lobbed their bombs over the fire-bay while the latter rushed the traverse ready to deal with any survivors who might have fight left in them, a dreadful attritional slogging match. Snipers were a constant and deadly menace. '10 January: The enemy started sniping us and when I got back to my trench I found Fryer had been shot dead. It gave me quite a nasty turn. I fear he had been looking up and had got an unlucky shot.'

No battalion spent all its time in the trenches. Service in the line was followed by a period in reserve, punctuated by welcome, if all too brief, spells of relative repose. Hilton observed that a poor billet merited more censure than an ill-sited or badly finished trench: '12 January: The billet in the convent isn't all that could be desired. It is strange how one exclaims over a bare room when one has been in the open.' Minor inconveniences in the daily attrition of death and disease often rankled: '17 January: Had to do the cooking as my new servant has gone sick. Troops are not standing this bad weather.' Out of the line periods in support or even at rest were marked by drill, parades and sport: '26 January: Had a company parade this morning near the asylum, something for the men to do; football match in the evening and paid out the men.'

Death in battle was not the only hazard. Major actions were relatively rare but random shelling, sniping and sheer bad luck ensured a steady flow of casualties whenever the battalion was 'up': '18 January: We had a very bad time today, the Germans shelled all day; I lost one killed and four wounded. The *minen-werfers* were very busy and about thirty of them fell in and around my trenches but did little damage, beyond frightening one platoon'.

An indispensable feature of the trench-fighter's troglodyte existence was the dugout. Generally, this limited accommodation was reserved for officers whilst ORs had to scrape shelters or 'funk-holes' in the sides of the trench. In the stygian, rat-infested gloom of the dugout, small comforts carried great weight: '20 January: saw a very neat stove today and have sent to Army & Navy Stores for one, hope it will arrive in time for our next go of trenches.' Happily it did: '4 February: Found my little primus stove very useful.'

Mail order was not always necessary. Parcels from home were a way for family and friends to remind soldiers that they were missed and cared for. Collecting and paying for comforts became a national activity. Businesses were quick to pick up on the trend. Adverts for morphine ampoules, complete with syringes, were placed by Boots the Chemist, whilst newspapers abounded with ads for useful gadgets like that primus stove, preparations to kill lice and tinned cakes.

During the third week of February the KOSB marched up to Ypres: '28 February: I went to 38 & 39 trenches this time. The Germans shelled us all day but only wounded one man. We had to work like niggers to get the trenches in any sort of order. The communication trench was awful.' By mid-March an attack on high ground near St. Eloi was being proposed but did not proceed. They did not entirely escape the attentions of the Kaiser's increasingly potent air force: 12 April: 'Zeppelins came over last night and dropped about half a dozen bombs. We could distinctly see the thing. The bombs did no damage at all.'

Within a month, they were being readied for an attack on Hill 60. This feature was entirely man made, a conical mound of spoil, left from railways construction. The heap rises some 60 metres; forming an artificial spur to the Messines Ridge where the first British mine of the war was blown by Lt. White RE on 17 February 1915. From the beginning of March, 173rd

The **CLEANEST** fighter in the World—
the British Tommy

The clean, chivalrous fighting instincts of our gallant soldiers reflect the ideals of our business life. The same characteristics which stamp the British Tommy as the *CLEANEST FIGHTER IN THE WORLD* have won equal repute for British Goods.

SUNLIGHT SOAP is typically British. It is acknowledged by experts to represent the highest standard of Soap Quality and Efficiency. Tommy welcomes it in the trenches just as you welcome it at home.

£1,000 GUARANTEE OF PURITY ON EVERY BAR.

The name Lever on Soap is a Guarantee of Purity and Excellence.

LEVER BROTHERS LIMITED, PORT SUNLIGHT.

A 1915 advert for Sunlight Soap, directly appealing to families back home wanting to send useful gifts to their loved ones on the front line. (The War Budget, via Wikimedia Commons)

Tunnelling Company, RE, had begun digging a series of three tunnels beneath the enemy line. It was filthy, dangerous and exhausting work, the tunnellers regularly disinterring the rotting remains of French and German dead. The explosion timed for 19.05 on 17 April flung a vast column of debris into the spring skies and the British attack swept forward, killing or capturing the shocked and stunned defenders for, by 1915 standards, very modest loss.

'17 April: Lay low in the communication trench and dugouts all day, in the evening the mines were exploded and I have never seen such a sight in my life, it was indescribable. The attack came off a few minutes later and off we went to the top of the hill and worked like niggers to make it defendable. At about midnight I retired to the woods and slept for about four hours.' The KOSB were not long in reserve. Despite the swiftness of the initial British success, the Germans, as ever, put in strong and determined counter-attacks: '18 April: Had to go and reinforce as the enemy were putting in a counter-attack. It was very difficult holding on. Command of the regiment devolved on me as all the seniors were killed or wounded. Marched off around 15.00 hours – very lucky to be alive!'

Any elation at such a significant success was diluted by knowledge of the blood price paid. Besides there was no respite, a major German offensive was brewing: '22 April: Had orders to occupy trenches 35 to 37 tonight. Marched off around 19.30 hours but when nearing Vlamertinge met the adjutant of the West Kents who had turned back and said the village was impassable on account of refugees. The French had given way and were running; the Germans had broken through.'

In early April, the British had taken over a further 5 miles of French-held trenches, north-east of the battered ruin of Ypres and it was here the blow fell. This, the second battle of Ypres, witnessed the first use of poison gas by the Germans on the Western Front. French colonial forces, faced with the satanic yellowish mist, broke. Canadians, deployed around St. Julien, did not and fought on in a display of sublime courage for which they paid a very heavy price.

In the wake of this break-in the situation in the salient deteriorated rapidly '23 April: About 14.00 hours we were ordered to stand to. We marched to the [Yser] Canal having been given orders for an attack at 16.15 hours or thereabouts. The men behaved splendidly. I finally decided I must push up to the firing line but didn't get far before I was bowled over. Broster pulled me into a ditch and I made my way to the dressing station. I was sent off to Poperinghe and from there to Boulogne.'

Although a bullet remained lodged in his spine for thirty years, Hilton returned to duty in 1916 and held a range of staff appointments, surviving the war without further injuries.

Baptism of fire

Despite initial German successes, Second Ypres quickly became a slogging match. The enemy blundered forward and the Allies blundered in riposte. General Smith-Dorrien was one high-ranking casualty, not of German bullets but of Sir John French's animosity. He had been foolish enough to suggest shortening the line at Ypres and avoiding further piecemeal and bloody counter-attacks. When General Plumer, his successor, suggested the same tactics, French concurred.

These finer points of grand tactics and general politicking were not immediately evident to Herbert Waugh and those other youthful Hectors who ventured across the Channel. Their expectation was that the damsels of France and Belgium would be lining up to surrender their favours. In this they would be disappointed. Tommy found the forward areas devoid of females and those he met in lanes and billets to the rear proved less than glamorous: 'Such girls as he encountered wore clogs, dressed like agricultural labourers, smelt of stables and byres and looked with reserve and suspicion at anything in a khaki uniform'.

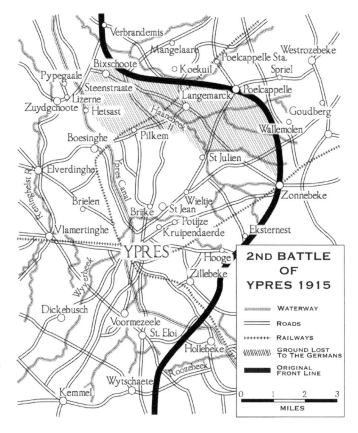

The battalion colonel was a figure of awe. The fusiliers 'gazed up at him as he clattered by on his great horse and asked each other if it was true that his monocle was affixed to the peak of his service cap by a hinge. One of his sayings was "a barrage moves as a pillar of cloud by day and fire by night". He had a marked aversion to any officer "not quite out of the right drawer" and, on encountering an officer in the trenches who had several days' growth of beard; he was heard to enquire "who is that officer with a face like a musical box?"'

The Geordies saw their first French *poilu* on the dockside at Boulogne; he 'stood silently on guard duty, cloaked and with a long bayonet fixed to his rifle.' Northern France, the first alien shore most had visited, was 'pretty, quite flat'. Billets were found in ancient timber framed-barns, for the most part dilapidated. St. George's Day 1915 was commemorated as the regiment's annual fete day, with officers sporting red and white roses. Marching ever nearer to the inferno, hobnails ringing on unyielding pave, they passed into Belgium where streams of refugees crowded the roads. As they neared Poperinghe, long toiling columns of wounded appeared. Men bloodied, vacant and broken, thrown out of the giant mincer of the Western Front as surely as they were now being drawn in. By Vlamertinghe, their trenches were real, wet and very cold at night. Waugh shared his billet with a friend, known as Broncho 'after a popular American western movie character'. The pair adopted the expedient of alternately using each other as a mattress, sharing body warmth. This was necessity rather than passion and permitted a measure of sleep.

As for their Belgian hosts, the fastidious Waugh observed; 'our allies serve an admirable cup of coffee but not always in a clean cup'. Battle-scarred Ypres was unrecognisable as the pleasing and prosperous medieval city it had been, 'the true tragedian, the Hamlet of them all – shells rattled over our heads like railway trains. We alternately walked and ran, stumbling over obstacles whilst fragments of roofing trickled down on us.'

In rain-soaked fields, heavy, cloying earth wet and pungent, backlit by the flames of burning villages, like some travesty of northern lights, the dipping arcs of flares ahead marked the front line. Next day, moving up they saw their first dead man, heard the first frantic calls for 'stretcher bearers'. Their home for 25 April was a 'muddy ditch' scarcely worth defining as a trench; next door, a British field battery whose constant roaring bark filled their senses. With every hour, the reality of the war intruded further:

> There was an ugly field to be crossed that morning, great shells plunging into all parts of it and throwing black fountains of earth

house-high. We wavered for a bit until the adjutant came up; 'come along "A" Company, they're not firing at you'; shrapnel and 'Jack Johnson's' falling all around us.

More shallow scrapes than trenches with little cover from snipers who now began to make themselves felt: walking wounded, 'dirty, disordered and exhausted' staggered by in droves. As morning wore on, fire from the heavier guns diminished, replaced by 'an increasing tattoo of small arms'. The almost reassuring business of digging in took on a new urgency. Labours were interrupted by a wild, dishevelled officer from the front who implored them 'to go up there'. The man was clearly in shock and the Fusiliers felt they had lost 'that boy-scout-on-holiday feeling'.

The morning of 26 April was to be 6th Battalion's moment of baptism. They went over attacking towards St. Julien; 'up the rise we began to meet machine-gun bullets in streams, rifle bullets from every angle and then the HE coal boxes or Jack Johnsons. 6th & 7th Battalions advanced towards the outskirts of the village where week old German dead lay all around.' More digging in – 'a hundred yards away the farmer lies dead amidst his roasted cattle, dead horses everywhere'.

To these young men drawn from their desks and dusty precedents, their comrades from regular battalions seemed like a breed apart. Tommies (Manchesters) and turbaned warriors of the Indian Army (Pathans) deployed alongside, seemed moulded into uniform, bearing the weight of their kit as though it weighed nothing at all, 'expressionless faces and listless gait, war's chloroform; one pitied the Indians especially, brown faces and gentle, lustrous dark eyes who had come so far to fight the white man's battles'.

'Individuals while abroad cannot well forget that they are foreigners, but battalions are communities and take their native atmosphere with them, like nomadic tribes'. Broncho, the Hollywood lookalike, 'an athletic public schoolboy, already qualified as a solicitor' who had drafted Waugh's will told his friend '"I've said goodbye to all the old life at home," so sure he was of his presentiment of impeding death, all too soon fulfilled; he was from Benton but never saw Benton again.'

The attack against St. Julien was hastily planned, ground not reconnoitred. Men moved forward beneath a full weight of kit, greatcoats included, much of which was jettisoned. They carried the older, Long Lee Enfield rifle, only field caps, no 'steel bowlers'. Many officers still carried pre-war private purchase rifles, originally intended for rather less dangerous sport. 'A brigade staff officer, red hat and all, galloped up to our company commander in tremendous haste, reined in his horse, shouted brief and urgent orders, pointed ahead with out-flung arm and rode off as quickly as he had come.' These Saturday night soldiers advanced towards contact 'and on we went, clerks, artisans and labourers led by solicitors, chartered accountants and land-agents, all dressed up in khaki'.

'The enemy played his complete orchestra, HE, Machine-gun and rifle fire'. The Fusiliers passed over the forward line, held by a Scottish unit, filing through a gap in the British wire and into no man's land. 'I remember P dropped his pipe, and popped back to pick it up – the enemy were invisible, lining the hedges in front, just like a sham attack in training. We were ordered to fire and to fix bayonets, advancing in rushes. All around the great black cones of blown up earth that rose out of the green plain, the whip-crack of bullets passing overhead and the little throbs as they hit the turf … during a moment's lull the sound of a lark in full song above.'

As the City Battalion struggled forward into the wall of enemy fire, Waugh was hit, 'a dull and heavy thump, a blow, and imagined for a minute I'd been struck by a flying stone'. He lay out on the field with other wounded and dead nearby: 'Z asked me to give a message to his mother in Byker'. Despite his own wounds Waugh complied. Three months later on returning to duty at the city's drill hall, he was astonished to see the same man very much alive, though walking with a stick.

Waugh was able to make his own way back to the regimental aid post, crammed into a disused stretch of trench. Another wounded comrade whose personal camera had somehow survived the fight offered to take photos – 'battle into bank holiday'. Having been patched up and still on his feet, Waugh was advised to make his way back into the ruins of what had been St. Jean. Sporadic shelling continued, rounds crashing among the waving trees. 'If I were you,' the MO cautioned as he set off, 'I'd avoid the trees there, it's by the cemetery and they're shelling it'. Having no wish to add to the graveyard population, Waugh took a more circuitous route to relative safety.

At a field ambulance station he was fed with warm, sweet tea, Tommy's universal remedy, bread and marmalade. A hazardous series of lifts by various conveyances eventually saw him back to Vlamertinghe. Painted images of long-dead saints flickered by candlelight as they gazed benignly down on scores of British wounded in an overcrowded church, huddled on chairs, prone on stretchers.

When the survivors of 149 Brigade were relieved next day, they had lost their commanding officer (Brigadier-General Riddell), 42 officers and 1,912 other ranks, roughly two thirds of their total strength. They were the first of the Territorials to go into action as a full brigade. Kitchener had been wrong – these unlikely soldiers had not faltered and had paid the full, terrible price of their blood passage.

Attrition

In the early weeks of 1915 a split had opened between the 'westerners' who perceived that the war would be lost and won on the Western Front and those who favoured a more peripheral or 'eastern' strategy. This was tried and tested and the easterners possessed impressive advocates in Churchill and Lloyd George. Kitchener wrote to French on 1 January indicating the easterners might get their way. The 'Little' Field Marshal was aghast; weakening the Western Front to create nothing more than a holding garrison would, in his view be disastrous. Of course the easterners got their way. The tragedy at Gallipoli became the graveyard of their hopes.

British attempts to break the deadlock of the trenches comprised attacks at Neuve Chapelle (10–13 March), at Aubers Ridge on 9 May and a fresh attempt at Festubert between 10 and 25 May. Despite some gains, all of these largely stalled with heavy losses. Massive firepower was not complimented by advanced communications. Telephone wires were soon cut and battalion runners struggling through a hell of ruined trenches and shell-lashed no man's land could not hope to provide commanders with fluid and accurate action reports. Ground gained was soon lost to counter-attacks. Allied operations were temporarily derailed when the Germans attacked at Ypres, a seesaw slogging match of positions lost and re-taken, only to be lost again. Despite this murderous baptism, many Saturday night soldiers still managed to churn the horror into verse, such as this anonymous verse:

> The Fiery cross is out, now
> There's a beacon on each hill,
> The Scottish pipes are sounding,
> 'Tis the slogan wild and shrill
> The Call of the Pipes
> I heard the bugles callin' an' join I felt I must,
> Now I wish I'd let them, go on blowin' till they bust!

Cavalry, the essence of exploitation, could no longer be effectively deployed. Whatever criticisms could be and have been launched against Allied generals, the fact remains that the deadlock simply could not, at this stage in the war, be broken. French attacks in Artois fared even worse and at terrible cost. When the British attack at Aubers Ridge foundered – as did the French offensive – broken against the deepening fortress of the German defence,

French, Joffre and Haig visit the front line 1915 (from GWS – The Great War: The Standard History of the All Europe Conflict *(volume four), 1915, via Wikimedia Commons)*

the relative weakness of Allied artillery was starkly highlighted. Lack of ammunition, in terms of type, quantity and quality, became a temporary cause célèbre and the 'shell scandal' brought Asquith's tottering ministry to its knees, ushering in the wartime coalition. Lloyd George took up responsibility for munitions. Nonetheless, lack of shells contributed to the British failure at Festubert in May.

Despite these repeated disappointments and the immense tide of casualties, French and Joffre, when they met at Chantilly on

24 June, remained wedded to further action along the Western Front. In this they were correct. The war would not be won on other, peripheral fronts but the price of victory would be very high indeed. Joffre pushed for an attack by Haig's First Army at Loos, the British having now extended their own lines eastwards into the dense mining belt of Artois. This was a fit setting for Germinal, a dense, bleak patchwork of collieries and huddled townships, slagheaps erupting over the largely flat ground like satanic sores. Haig was not impressed: 'most unfavourable ground'. French shared his subordinate's concerns. 'Papa' Joffre was insistent and received unexpected support from Kitchener himself, committed on account of the Russians' deteriorating position in the east to do whatever must be done to aid the French, even though heavy losses became inevitable.

From 25 September to the night of 13/14 October the battle of Loos consumed 43,000 British casualties. Despite prodigies of valour – none more Homeric than Piper Daniel Laidlaw of 7th Battalion, KOSB, leading the fight for Hill 70 on the first day – the battle achieved little. The strategic balance was unaffected. Field Marshal French's career was another casualty. His position had steadily crumbled throughout 1915 and Haig had unashamedly been jockeying for his job. He fully exploited his influence with the king to undermine his commanding officer. Their final meeting on 18 December, by which time French was all too painfully aware of how he had been intrigued against and betrayed, was far from cordial.

Hang on and hope

Sergeant Robert Constantine served in 9th Battalion, DLI. Born in Newcastle in 1887, he had enlisted at the age of 23. He served at Second Ypres and wrote to his brother, Jim, from Potijze on 13 May:

After nine days nice rest we are back again in the trenches and it's hell all day long, shells of all sorts bursting about but the German shells are not very good because I've seen a lot of them not burst at all and others are full of marbles and some of our chaps were saying they had seen some burst that were full of nails, a nice thing to put in shells, eh? I put in an awful day in yesterday, it was the longest day I've ever had and I felt properly upset and could not get a bit nap at all.

Already, those who had 'cushy' jobs back home were becoming objects of envy: 'Tell Ben Hodgson he should be very thankful to be where he is, I would just like to change places with him now! We passed a large city on Tuesday night on our way to the trenches and the whole place from end to end was on fire, what a sight, it's just done for wilful destruction and nothing else. We all know about "Lusitania" but have not seen the papers with any of the news yet … You shouldn't grumble about going to bed without a light, you should be lucky you have such a nice bed, I know I would just now.'

John Walcote Gamble, originally a native of Derbyshire, volunteered with the Public Schools Battalion at Ashtead in Surrey, transferring firstly to 16th Battalion, DLI but actually serving with the 14th. He went to France in October 1914 and served till he was wounded on 8 January 1916. He wrote to his family on 23 October, describing life in the trenches that autumn: 'In our company mess (there are six of us) we do have some cakes, and also a few extras which we are able with difficulty to get from villages nearby, such as tinned fruit, salmon or sardines and vegetables … A three-days-old newspaper usually drags through but I shall always be glad to get papers or magazines of any description.'

The network of *estaminets* which would be so crucial to the comfort of men in the trenches was starting to be established by this time. People who had lost their living to the fighting now began to provide services for troops running small cafés where Tommy could try exotic delights like *vin blanc* for the first time. One Belgian dish really caught on and was taken home: egg and chips.

Life in the trenches was uncongenial:

> We are in these alleged trenches for a week, and hope to get relieved on Sunday night. They are more breastworks than trenches, and are by no means sound. We spend all spare time strengthening and repairing them. At one point we are right up close to the Germans and can hear them quite plainly at times. It rained hard last night and the 'ditches' were in a frightful mess this morning, literally over the boot tops in mud everywhere. I think, considering that the British have held them for many months, that the regiments who have been in before ought to have seen to it, that they were well-drained, bomb-proof and comfortable long ago.
>
> I suppose the explanation is that one regiment only occupies this part of the line for a short period at a time and they don't like wasting time improving trenches for someone else's benefit. The last lot the 14th [DLI] were in were absolutely top notch, properly drained, boarded and concreted, and in every way comfortable and safe; but you see a Territorial Brigade had been there for two months and taken real pains to get their quarters jolly good.

On 20 November, Second Lieutenant Gamble acquainted his readers with a new parody of *Little Grey Home in the West*:

> There's a shallow wet trench near Houplines
> 'Tis the wettest there ever has been,
> There are bullets that fly,
> There are shells in the sky,
> And it smells like a German 'has been'.
>
> My dug-out's a haven of rest,
> Though it's only a tumble down nest,
> But with 'Johnsons' around,
> I must keep underground,
> Till the golden sun sinks in the west.

Humour masked a dank, exhausting and unendingly miserable existence with the added zest of constant danger:

It was intensely cold; the hail came across with such force that it seemed to be mixed with bullets and I'm sure many men must have thought they were shot by hail-stones. The harder we pumped, the deeper the water seemed to become. If we had left it undisturbed, we should have been frozen in and the Boche was rather active with his artillery. We discussed various ways of using or abusing the liquid devil. One bright idea was to cut a trench through from our line to theirs, make it fairly deep, run in the water and torpedo them! Boat and swimming races were dismissed as frivolous but the idea of skating about the support trenches was seriously considered!

Getting out proved as hazardous as staying in:

There were great rejoicings when we were relieved yesterday morning at dawn, although we had quite an exciting time getting out; you see we usually empty about half a dozen communication trenches along the line but on this occasion only one was really safe from drowning casualties. It was an extremely tedious business getting a battalion out by one route and we could not get started till after the appointed time, owing to the relieving people meeting with similar difficulties.

As winter deepened, the harsh weather continued, sliding into deep cold. Opportunities for relief were few, even shell-shattered Ypres proved a slight diversion. Gamble recorded in his letter of 23 December: 'On Saturday then I took advantage of the temporary calm, and had another look round Ypres. It is really a wonderful sight – weird, grotesque, and desolate of course, but most interesting. I expect the place will be flooded with sight-seers and tourists after the war, and they will be amazed by what they see. The ancient ruins of Pompeii and such places will be simply out of it.' The following day, Sunday, was rather far from restful:

About 05.30, I was aroused in my dug-out by a gas-helmeted and scared sentry, the sound of voluminous rifle fire and big guns, and above all a choking feeling. Our dug-out was already full of gas, and for a moment the terror of waking up to such a situation properly put the wind up both Eyre (who shared my dug-out) and me. I could not at first find my gas helmet, and began to splutter and choke, but eventually I got it fixed on, and went out to get to business at once. And how terrible it was! The gas was rolling across towards us in thick whitish-yellow clouds; men were running about with their weird-looking gas-helmets on, and shells were bursting all around. It was, of course, quite dark and, as each shell burst, it caused a tremendous crash and a horrible flash of fire.

As I emerged from my dug-out there seemed to be a hundred big shells bursting, lighting up everything. The noise of all these tons of high explosives bursting all around was almost unbearable, and then to put the tin hat on it, every British gun in the vicinity began to pound away at top speed. It took me some time to realise what was happening but I soon got information and orders that there was a gas attack on in the front line and we were to man the reserve trenches at once. A number of men were already gassed, but we got into those trenches amid a huge bombardment and expected to see the Boche coming across at any moment. The men began to stifle and choke, and the shells were doing a great deal of damage amongst our troops but they stuck it wonderfully. The gas still came over in great clouds and the shelling continued unceasingly.

They evidently anticipated a big attack as they were peppering all the roads, rails and communications up which reinforcements might be brought, and were simply battering our reserve position to nothing, they seemed to be using every big gun they had, and were sending over every kind of shell from a 17 inch down to a small whizz-bang. The noise was appalling and nerve wracking, and there was no cessation for three hours. Then the gas began

The Germans first used **chlorine gas** at Second Ypres and the Allies were totally unprepared. Early gas hoods were improvised, uncomfortable and disorientating to wear, proofed with acetone which was processed from conkers – a cash bonus for children who were paid to collect bags of them!

to thin and the shelling toned down, and the joyous news came through that our two companies in the front line had repulsed the first German attack.

Their ordeal was not yet over:

> We stood to all that Sunday morning, strained and waiting after 3½ hours under gas and shell-fire and without food, and then came the order for us to go up to the front trench to relieve the companies who had had a shocking time. We'd already had a lot of casualties and Willis was horribly wounded early on, and Iveson knocked out by shell-shock. Iveson had recovered splendidly by the time we went up into action however, and we'd just got the company formed up and were starting up the road from our reserve trenches, when we got a 'Jack Johnson' right into us and laid out a lot of good fellows. We had a nasty job getting right up, but we manned that front line, and were ready for the Huns coming over. They did not attack again on Sunday but we were on the watch all night and early the next morning, they gassed again, but we did not allow them to get into our trench, and all day Monday we potted away hard, until by the evening the show seemed about over…

Though the fury of attacks ebbed, gas and shells continued to arrive: 'They gave our line a furious strafing to finish up with though, and Eyre got two wounds in the hand and back, and another 16th officer, Hickson, had been gassed previously; well, we hung on until late that night, and then came out; of course getting shelled and machine-gunned coming out. We got back about 0200 hours on Tuesday. We had been without rest or food for nearly 48 hours; been under gas for over three hours at one time, and I just collapsed, but am alright again now, except for sickness and headache, owing to that devilish gas.' As ever in the maelstrom, odd anecdotal details stuck in the mind:

> I had just been bandaging up a couple of wounded, when one of them called my attention to a couple of big rats which were

One man and his dog. (From The Book of Dogs, *1919, via Wikimedia Commons)*

staggering about on their hind legs as though drunk. It really was one of the funniest sights imaginable. One usually gets only glimpses of rats as they scuttle rapidly by during the day, but these two were right out in the open, and their antics were too quaint. They were half-gassed of course but strangely enough it was one of the things I remembered best after the show was over – one good thing the gas did was to kill a lot of the little beasts!

1915 would be the year of stalemate. The plain fact was that mere flesh and blood could never get through barbed wire and machine guns. Industrial war was a game for the well-dug-in defender. The Germans were very good at digging in.

CHAPTER 3

ATTRITION

1916

At the Chantilly conference in December 1915, Haig and Joffre had discussed ideas for joint offensives in 1916. Haig was by no means confident of his ally's capacity to do more and was increasingly (and correctly) of the view that Britain must shoulder the greater burden. A week before Verdun furiously erupted, the two commanders met again. The concept of a major joint offensive astride the River Somme was, at least in general terms, agreed with a proposed start date of 1 July. Haig was not a fan of the Somme area. Strategically it had little to offer. As ever, he preferred to look toward Flanders.

Verdun, the cauldron, changed all this. Without Haig's full support it was feared the French would crumble. When, on 26 May, Haig informed his ally that his New Army divisions would not be ready till perhaps August, Joffre was appalled. The French, he expostulated, might very well not survive that long. Haig rather drily observed that a fine vintage brandy calmed Joffre's Gallic nerves most admirably. That the British would attack in the Somme department was now a given. Haig's misgivings were secondary to his need to prop up Britain's ally before the weight of German blows proved too much.

The Plan

General Henry Rawlinson, leading Fourth Army, now held the right of the British line and the brunt of the coming battle would be borne by divisions under his command. The fight would be spread over a front of some 20 miles, across the deceptively mild chalk downs of Picardy, from Foncquevillers in the north to Mericourt in the south where the British and French sectors would intersect on the line of the River Somme. The Somme is probably the best known of all World War I battles; as with Verdun for the French, it symbolises the loss of a generation, a frightful gobbling up of blood and manhood for seemingly trifling gains.

Along the otherwise insignificant ridge running from Thiepval to Ginchy the Germans had turned sleepy hamlets into bristling fortresses: Serre, Thiepval, La Boisselle and Fricourt. Their front line studded with strong redoubts, with successive belts riding the crests of ridges behind, like spume on breakers, each a major tactical problem in itself. Chalk, firm and clear to Tommies after the mud and slop of Flanders, was ideal for carving deep dugouts, the enemy line was immensely strong and utterly formidable. Rawlinson himself was an advocate of 'bite and hold'; a series of limited assaults, each quickly consolidated and then built up in readiness for the next. Haig needed rather more. He had to have breakthrough, a smashing of the enemy line and a clear run for his cavalry to Bapaume, up the dead straight Roman road from Albert.

Rawlinson diplomatically, if with reservations, bowed to his superior's wishes but insisted on massive, drenching bombardment as a necessary prelude. A continuous deluge of fire so utterly overwhelming it would crush the enemy front-line defences to dust and decimate the troops holding it. Kitchener's New Army men would be the main attacking force and it was feared their training was insufficient to instil complex 'fire and movement' tactics. Instead, they would move forward from their start lines in four orderly waves, rifles sloped and walk towards the enemy front line, which would simply be theirs for the taking.

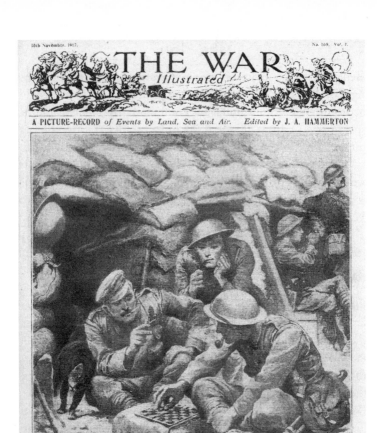

18th November. 1917.

No. 169. Vol. 7.

THE WAR
Illustrated

A PICTURE-RECORD *of Events by Land, Sea and Air.* *Edited by* J. A. HAMMERTON

TRENCH STRATEGISTS. British soldiers enjoy a game of draughts during a period of comparative inaction in a front-line trench. In such games the men find occasional relief from the tedium of waiting, when the fighting is for a time limited to that of the artillery. Despite the shells passing overhead, the men are yet able to concentrate their attention on the minor strategy of their pastime.

'Trench strategists', note the newly introduced Brodie helmets, pictured in
The War Illustrated, *November 1917. (Author's collection)*

Charles Moss, a lance corporal commanding a Lewis gun section of the Durham Pals, was very much a product of the radical tradition. He was scathing about the direction of the war and the scant regard paid to the efforts of the PBI:

Dispatches sent by war correspondents to the censored capitalist press never did justice, or give reasonable insight into the actions of the rankers ... how we used to laugh and scoff at the War Office threadbare communiqué 'All Quiet on the Western Front'. We knew that during the period covered by the communiqué, there had been terrific bombardments, bombing raids, fighting patrols, wiring parties, trench digging, mine-tunnelling and many other dangerous activities, especially at night that meant hard work, constant courage, ceaseless vigilance, disciplined conduct, the loss of life and limb...

Our battalion was in reserve, with the exception of 'D' Company, part of 93rd Brigade, 31st Division commanded by General Sir Aylmer Hunter-Weston. The other battalions in the Brigade were the Leeds and Bradford Pals of West Yorkshire Regiment. The Leeds Pals with our own 'D' Company were to be the first wave over the top followed at half-hour intervals by the Bradfords and then our battalion with the object of holding that part of the line captured by the West Yorks. It was to be our job to consolidate the position against German counter-attacks. Our 'D' Company had a special job in the first wave to link the Leeds Pals with the Seaforth Highlanders on our right. 'D' Company had a special objective, to capture the fortified position called Pendant Copse. The sector of our attack was in front of the village of Collincamps and nearly opposite to Beaumont Hamel held by the Germans: our Division had done the trench duties and worked on this part of the front, digging telephone and assembly trenches since we arrived from Egypt in April 1916.

Their training had at least not been completely neglected: 'We did not know that we were preparing for an attack until we had a sort of rehearsal of the plan and method of attack a few weeks before the time to "go over". A miniature copy of the German trenches had been prepared for this purpose on the open country a few miles behind our billets. A few brass hats explained the plan of attack, the timing of the attacking waves, the control of the artillery barrage and the formation of each battalion wave. Then each battalion practised their part in it.' Charles Moss was no respecter of fools and maintained a healthy disdain for those above who knew not what they did:

I was shown exactly where my Lewis gun post was to be but when I asked the officer what my field of fire would be like he couldn't tell me. I pointed out that the sort of country in front was the most vital thing for me to deal with enemy counter attacks, he resented my calling his attention to this, and all he could say was that I would find that out when we got there. I thought that was a poor lookout when so much depended upon this very necessary information and told him so.

There was to be two sets of distinguishing marks to be included in our equipment. All ranks of the West Yorks would have a triangle shaped piece of tin, cut from empty biscuit tins, fastened to their backs, so that the airmen who were going to watch the progress of the attack from the air, would be able to recognise our men and report to HQ how the attack was going. Also each man had a few pieces of coloured tape fastened to his shoulder straps and hanging down his back so that the battalions would be able to recognise each other as no regimental badges or numerals were to be worn. Each colour represented the colour that had been given as a name to the trench they were to capture.

It was essential that the bombardment should not only crush the Germans huddled in their deep dugouts but it should also cut those dense belts of barbed wire. In many instances the shells failed to do their work. Those who had doubts, and there were many, including Rawlinson, kept these to themselves and permitted no mutterings by others. The deadly equation was defined as 'the race for the parapet'. If the attackers could cross no man's land and occupy front-line enemy trenches before those defenders who survived could bring their weapons, particularly their machine guns, into action then they would win the day. If not they would be decimated.

The start of the attack had been fixed for June 28th but it rained so heavily for about a week before that, despite the terrific bombardment by our artillery, most of the German barbed wire entanglements were still as strong as ever on the 28th. These barbed wire defences were a great wonder to me; all the daring hard work that had been put into them. They were a great, massive rusty wire wall built along the whole of the Western Front. They were about five or six feet high and three to four yards deep in most places built up on strong wooden and iron stakes, the German wire always looked a far better job than ours, the Jerries were out working on their wire every night. Every break our artillery made in their wire during the day, they repaired during the night, and on June 28th their wire was still as strong, despite our terrific and long bombardment that the attack was put off until July 1st... It was impossible to get any sleep during the night because of a heavy, long-distance battery and a great howitzer belching all night long.

We were on fatigues during the day, carrying ammunition and 'plum-pudding' mortar shells to dumps near the front line. The shells were brutes to carry. They were about the size of a football with a steel shank attached. Many of these never reached the drops because many of the carriers, to save themselves from struggling down the trench with them, just tipped them into the deep gullies that crossed the communication trenches, everybody remained in good spirits despite all the rain and mud and bad feeding arrangements and the filthy and verminous condition we were all in.

Charles Moss' platoon officer, Lieutenant Simpson, had asked the lance corporal to volunteer for a night-time mission out into no man's land where he and the subaltern would attempt to report on the state of German wire. As he'd been on exhausting supply duty all day, Moss was excused, though pleased his officer reposed so much confidence in him, 'it would have been a miracle if we'd got back alive'. During Friday 30th, the battalion took up positions in the line south of Collincamps, finding rough and ready billets in 'the ruins of a badly strafed chateau'. In the evening their CO briefed the Durhams on their role in the forthcoming attack:

> There was to be no turning back, every man must advance at a steady pace. All officers had authority to shoot anyone who stopped or tried to turn back. The wounded had to be left to be attended to by the stretcher bearers and RAMC. The grimmest order to me

A Casualty in the Red Cross Canine Contingent

French Red Cross dog having his wounded paw dressed by an Army doctor. This dog, struck by a stray bullet while searching for wounded behind the firing-line, wears an expression of patient optimism, almost as though aware that he had suffered in his country's cause. Dogs play very useful parts with the French Army, some as sentries and others as Red Cross helpers. In this latter capacity it is their duty to search for wounded men who may have been overlooked, possibly through having crawled into undergrowth. When the dogs find a soldier they take his kepi or something else belonging to him, and hurry back with it to the ambulance workers

A casualty in the Canine contingent, The War Illustrated, *January 1916. (Author's collection)*

was that no fighting soldier was to stop to help the wounded. The CO was very emphatic about this. It seemed such a heartless order to come from our CO who was a Brigadier-General of Church Lads Brigades and looked upon as a religious man, (I thought bringing in the wounded was how Victoria Crosses were won). We spent the rest of the evening being issued with field dressings, extra ammunition, picks and shovels, camouflaging our tin hats with scraps of sandbag and sharpening bayonets.

That evening, in the deepening dusk, the Durhams marched via a railways hollow to the communication trench, 'called Eczema all the time we had used it for front line duties but it had been renamed Southern Avenue for the purposes of the attack'. German artillery was zeroed on the entrance and the Tommies had to dash between shell-bursts. 'We could see in a lurid glow, sections of troops moving slowly forward towards the trenches. The whole awesome scene was lifted so much above reality to me that, although some of us were setting out to be killed, wounded, taken prisoner or to win glory none of those thoughts entered my head. I was too fascinated by the mightiness of the spectacle … I had no thoughts for anything else.' Merely reaching the front line was both hard and tiring for the over-laden Tommies:

> It was slow and hard work to get along that Railway Trench, we so often had to fling ourselves down in the trench to avoid the shrieking shells. When we reached the entrance to Southern Avenue, the area was so crowded with troops that it was some time before we got into it. It was marvellous how each section kept together in such a mix up. We were all carrying so much it was like a free-fight to move at all.
>
> Over and above our ordinary equipment, rifle, ammunition and bayonet, I had a khaki bandolier full of .303 [calibre] six loaded Lewis Gun magazines carried in a horse's nose-bag because we hadn't enough proper containers available, two Mills Bombs and a pick with the shaft stuck down behind my haversack and we were called 'light' infantry! But most ironical of all was the dirty tricks our clumsy bad fitting tin-hats played us; if the chin-strap wasn't trying to strangle us, the 'soup-basin' was falling over our eyes to blind us. Steel helmets always got more curses than blessings from us. After many stops and much struggling, falling down and getting caught in signallers' telephone wires we reached our assembly trench at about 4 a.m. on Saturday 1st July.

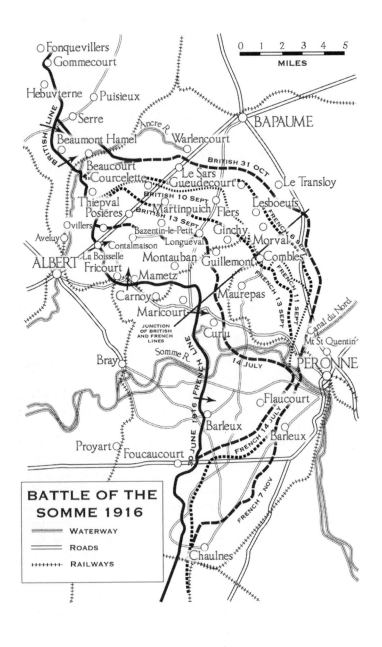

Fonquevillers
Gommecourt
Hebuterne
Puisieux
Serre
Ancre R.
Warlencourt
BAPAUME
BRITISH LINE
Beaumont Hamel
BRITISH 31 OCT
Beaucourt
Courcelette
Le Sars
Gueudecourt
Le Transloy
Thiepval
Posières
BRITISH 10 SEPT
Martinpuich
Flers
Lesboeufs
Ovillers
BRITISH 13 SEPT
Bazentin-le-Petit
Ginchy
FRENCH 16 SEPT
Aveluy
Contalmaison
Longueval
Morval
La Boiselle
Montauban
Combles
ALBERT
Fricourt
Guillemont
FRENCH 11 SEPT
Mametz
Maurepas
FRENCH 13 SEPT
Carnoy
Maricourt
JUNCTION
OF BRITISH
AND FRENCH
LINES
Curlu
Mt St Quentin
Canal du Nord
Bray
Somme R.
14 JULY
PÉRONNE
30 JUNE 1916 FRENCH LINE
Flaucourt
Barleux
Barleux
Proyart
Foucaucourt
FRENCH 14 JULY
FRENCH 7 NOV
**BATTLE OF THE
SOMME 1916**

▭▭▭ WATERWAY

──── ROADS

+++++++ RAILWAYS

Chaulnes

1 July 1916

Charles Moss and the Durham Pals were very near the front of the front as dawn broke:

> The trench was just a temporary assembly one, about four feet deep without any firestep or proper parapet. It was dug just to afford a bit of protection from machine-gun and rifle fire, while we waited to move to our jumping-off trench in readiness to go over. Most of us got into the assembly trench in pretty fair condition. Our artillery was blazing away, a terrific bombardment of the German lines. The Germans themselves were comparatively quiet until about 6 a.m. they must have waited till we were all in position, then they opened up on us with all they had and in every calibre. There was no need for them to do any range-finding; they were dead on our front at once. Along on my left, there was soon word being passed along for stretcher bearers.
>
> We heard that several of our company had been hit by their first salvo; the trench was so shallow I was having to crouch low into the front of it but, regardless of the danger, Lieutenant Simpson kept moving up and down the trench with his head and shoulders in full view of the Germans. I told him he was 'asking for it' but he took no notice and kept on having a word here and there with the fellows while we waited. At 7.30 a.m. – Zero Hour time for the first wave to go over, we heard a great heavy rumbling thud which was the exploding of our great mine. This mine is recorded in the official account as being the greatest mine that had ever been blown.

This flank of the attack from Serre to Beaumont Hamel was to prove disastrous and costly; producing no tangible gains though some of the Durham Pals did penetrate as far as Pendant Copse. A few even struggled through as far as the ruins of Serre. Without support, they were inevitably picked off.

> I wanted to see how our attack was going so I moved some of the chalk on the front of the trench in such a way that I could be protected from German sniper fire and took a good look at the

Mine explosion, 1916. (Agence Rol, Bibliothèque nationale de France, via Wikimedia Commons)

German line in front of us. But all that I could see was fountains of chalk and smoke sent up by our artillery barrage. It was like watching heavy seas roaring onto Hendon Beach as I have seen during winter storms. Whilst I was watching I saw the barrage lift and storm further back over the third German line. As it got clear of one of the German trenches, out onto the top came scrambling a German machine-gun team. They set up their gun in front of their parapet and opened up a slow and deadly fire on our front. The gunners were without their tunics and worked the gun in their shirt sleeves in quite a different manner to their usual short, sharp bursts. Their fire was so slow that every shot seemed to have a definite aim. Except for that gun team there wasn't another soldier either in British Khaki or German grey to be seen…

When we got into our jumping off trench I found it was in one of those deep hollows that were peculiar to this part of the front, and was called 'dead ground' because of the protection it afforded. Part of it was occupied by our battalion HQ. The CO & Adjutant were there. As soon as I got there I found out something had gone wrong with our procedure, because Lance Corporal Fletcher had been called away with No. 1 gun. The arrangement had been that No. 1 gun was to stay with HQ but as it had gone I had to remain with HQ with my gun. A little further along the trench there were some scaling ladders up which some of our fellows were climbing. 'Big Lizzie' – the nickname we had given this officer, was brandishing a revolver, shouting and urging them up the ladders. I watched this for a minute or two when down into the hollow came Corporal Forshaw, one of the battalion runners. He was very excited and was shouting as he came, something to the effect 'the whole show is a b***s up!'

The CO spoke to him but I could not hear what he said for the infernal row of the shell fire but the CO came near and shouted to 'Big Lizzie', 'wait a moment, Mr. ******* a minute or two will neither win nor lose this battle'. The officer at once stopped waving his revolver and stopped the fellows who were climbing the ladders, and then they all crouched down at the bottom of the trench. In that moment, along came an Army Corps runner and handed the CO an envelope. The CO opened it, read the message it contained and striking a dramatic attitude he turned to the Adjutant and said 'Ah, ah Mr. Lowes, this is where we come in' and he read the message; 'Your attack has failed, 18th DLI take over the front line from Point * to Point *'.

Had there been no confusion over the placing of the Lewis gun teams and had the runner not arrived, Charles Moss and his comrades would have gone over the top at that point and been shot to pieces as had so many of those who had gone before. The first day of the Somme, 1 July 1916, was the bloodiest in the history of the British Army. A total of 57,470 casualties were sustained, some 19,240 of these were fatalities. German machine guns did fearful execution and, with the exception of the southern part of the line, hardly any gains were made. Names such as Serre and Beaumont Hamel would be synonymous with bloody failure, made worse by the extreme heroism of Kitchener's civilian soldiers. Some like the 36th (Ulster) Division, north of Thiepval, fought like tigers and hacked out illusory gains, all briskly eliminated by powerful, local counter-attacks.

If Charles Moss had been temporarily spared, the Durham Pals still had a surfeit of woe ahead:

> The CO & Adjutant had a brief consultation, and then the CO gave 'Big Lizzie' an order to muster as many men as he could and occupy that part of the front line which had been allotted to us. The artillery fire was much quieter by the time we reached what had once been the front line trench but it was impossible to tell it from No-Man's-Land. Most of the revetting and fire-steps had been blown in. The whole of the front was an awful chaos of duck-boards, sandbags, and stakes, and wire netting, barbed wire and dud shells, tumbled and strewn about. It was impossible to recognise a revetment from a fire-bay. Amongst this awful wreck were the dead bodies of what appeared to be a Leeds Pals Lewis gun team, with their gun and drums of ammunition lying near them.
>
> One of my team picked up the Lewis gun and we took it with us making two guns for the rest of the time we were in the front line. One of these dead soldiers was a horrible sight; a shell must have burst so near to him that it had ripped all the uniform and flesh from the front of his body. I was surprised to see a black retriever roaming about but it disappeared down the remains of a dugout when we got near it. This dog was the only living thing we saw as we struggled along the front line.
>
> Most of the West Yorks and our 'D' Company had been killed or wounded in their assembly trenches on our sector during the intense bombardment before Zero Hour, this was coupled with the tactical mistake on our High Command's part in having a fixed time for the lifting of our artillery barrage from one German trench to the next after Zero which meant that when the barrage was lifted off the German second line it allowed them to bring their machine-guns out of their deep dugouts and fire them on top in comparative safety, while our barrage during that tragic half hour was concentrated for that fixed period on the German third line.

Moss and his comrades learned from the few survivors that the whole of the first three attacking waves had been decimated either prior to or immediately after zero hour. Many had not survived long enough even to get out of the British trenches. Scything machine-gun fire and a hurricane of shells had winnowed those who did.

> After seeing the dog disappear, my gun team and I kept on struggling along the trench past several bodies of West Yorks until we reached a position well to the left of the Lewis gun post I knew so well. I had been in charge of this post when we did our ordinary front line duties. It was at the corner of the road that led from Mailly-Mailly to Serre. This road was part of no man's land for some distance. It was about forty yards wide at this point and commanded by the famous German Quadrilateral Redoubt. The whole front had gone very quiet along here and, during the afternoon, I set up our Lewis gun a bit north of Roby Roy Communication trench not far from Fonquevillers...
>
> There was so few of us to hold this part of the line that I thought what a walkover the Jerries would have if they were to attack us. This was the only chance we had had to get anything to eat and I was especially thankful for a packet of 'Sunmaid' raisins I had received in a parcel I had from my sister in Winnipeg. Most of the food and water we got had a filthy taste because of all the chlorination there was in it but those raisins went down well with some of the hard wheaten biscuits that I liked to crunch so much. We had a reasonable rest until it was dark then we moved into No-Man's-Land and set up the Lewis guns in a shell-hole. To get into No-Man's-Land we had to pass one of those deep hollows with a few bushes growing in them. This one may have been St. John's or St. Paul's Copse. As we passed the place, we could hear many awful moans and agonised cries for stretcher-bearers coming from the depth of the hollow. Many of the badly wounded had managed to struggle into this place for protection from shell and machine-gun fire...

So ended the first day of the battle of the Somme, there were 140 left to go.

High summer

Rawlinson's idea – which, as Richard Holmes points out, was the novel one of reinforcing failure – involved more costly and fruitless attacks on those strongpoints where earlier costly and fruitless attacks had failed. In the south, opportunities beckoned. Attacks on 3 July did indeed gain ground though it took another nine bloody days to secure Mametz Wood. On 14 July, Fourth Army mounted a dazzling night attack with a full and effective bombardment. The infantry were preceded by a hurricane fire, brief but devastating. Significant gains were made for, by Somme standards, modest losses. This was bite and hold in the best sense but it was not a breakthrough. Far from it, those key areas of Delville and High Wood remained in German hands and the taking of both would be long drawn out and terrible.

Manning their outpost in no man's land during the night of 1/2 July, Charles Moss and his comrades had no leisure for pondering on grand tactics:

> The darkness of the night was often broken by brilliant glow from arching Verey lights being fired across No-Man's-Land. As each light died out, we were blinded, the darkness being deeper than ever. The sudden change from blackness to such weird and ghostly light thrown onto the tragic shapes of the charred stumps of trees whose tops had been blasted off during previous bombardments made the place such a terrible eerie sight, that I felt as though I was no longer on the civilised world.
>
> People have heard a lot about Hell, but no one has come back from there to tell us what it really is like. I know I was very near to it as the red light from the star shell and explosions fell on the hollow, whilst the cries of despair from the wounded mingled with the Devil's tattoo of rifle and machine-gun fire. We thought the Germans might send a bombing raid over so we'd had to struggle out into No-Man's-Land where we got into a big shell hole and set to with picks and shovels to make it into a Lewis gun post.
>
> One of my gunners 'got the wind up' very badly. He would dash himself from one side of the hole to the other at each shell-burst. I was urging him to keep still in the bottom of the hole when he gave a great gasp and groaned 'Death, oh death! They've knocked a bloody hole right through us'. He scrambled out of the shell-hole before anyone could help him and I saw no more of him till I

reached the 3rd Battalion at South Shields in 1917 where I found that the shrapnel had wounded him in the shoulder and given him a Blighty that got him to England.

Next morning the gun team had scrambled back to the wrecked front line and 'stood to' with the remainder of 'C' Company. Despite their fragile position, no attacks came. Charles and his comrades retired along a communication trench:

> This was one of the shelters that had been used as an advanced dressing station. The duckboards inside were covered with a horrible mixture of blood and chalk puddle, used field dressings and the remains of hurried operations. It looked so repulsive that we were hesitating about going inside when there was the crash of a 5.9 shell a bit further down the trench, the blast from it nearly blew us inside and as the strafe continued close by we went inside and thought it best to stay there. We shovelled out, as best we could, the shocking evidence of the suffering of the wounded and the harrowing work of the 'worst paid' (first aid) wallahs. Then we set about cleaning our rifles, Lewis Guns and ammunition drums…
>
> While we were in the shelter the talk amongst the team became very morbid and downhearted. They would persist in talking about the cruel and gruesome sights they had seen, and how easily such things could happen to them. One of the youngest, a lad of about 17, was becoming very distressed as the despondent talk continued. I realised I would have to get their minds onto other and more cheerful things, so when one of them passed the remark, that had become a favourite army saying when things were looking black, 'it's a bloody good job we've got a navy', I took this as my cue to turn the talk to ships and the sea. So I got them interested in some of my trips with the Merchant Navy, especially my trips to Europe on the Londonderry boats out of Seaham Harbour. It was marvellous how they responded to the change of subject, the young gunner brightened up considerably and the rest of them stopped their depressing gossip.

At Agincourt in October 1415, particularly glutinous Somme mud had slowed down heavily harnessed French men-at-arms as they slogged forward into the arrow storm. Five hundred years later the mud was the same: wet, slithering, and everywhere. A damp summer churned chalk into mire, a dismal humid season dominated by the incessant roar of the guns. Artillery was fast becoming dominant on the battlefield and though the British gunners had much to learn from their mistakes, they proved apt pupils. The Royal Flying Corps' local air superiority gave them clear eyes, though this was not necessarily apparent to those mud-caked and weary survivors of the Durham Pals.

Prevailing German tactical doctrine, hammered home to local commanders by Falkenhayn, was that ground must firstly be held at all costs and if lost, recovered at all costs. These grim summer battles of attrition cost both sides equally dear. In the course of this bitter, savage stalemate, Fourth Army sustained another 82,000 casualties, a butcher's bill undreamed of in previous conflicts. Waterloo, a very great battle by the standards of the day, cost the British and their allies 17,000 dead and wounded. The Somme would cost at least 27 times as many. For the moment, as the July offensive was resumed south of the Durhams' positions, Charles Moss and his gunners remained largely out of harm's way:

> At daylight on Tuesday morning we moved to the notorious Monk Trench. This trench was looked upon by our fellows as a suicide post because of the bad name it had for casualties while we were there on tours of duty. It was on a spur of high ground which overlooked the narrow part of No-Man's-Land. It was a favourite place for the Jerries to vent their hate in the shape of Minnies, coal-boxes and Whizz-bangs. The weather had been close and overcast all that time from Zero Hour but, as we reached this trench, there came of a terrific thunderstorm and deluge of rain which poured into the trenches from the higher ground and the trench was soon filling up with water.
>
> We had a setback right at the entrance to the trench, the man who was leading the gun-team backed away from a disembowelled body lying beside the firestep. I eventually led them into position where we found several of my platoon…
>
> The storm had increased so much that we had to climb onto the parados to save ourselves from the danger of drowning. We had put the Lewis guns on the parapet in ground sheets, the chalk was bouncing up, driven by the force of the rain. I was having to shake the guns clear of chalk to prevent them getting buried in it. To

have fired them would have been impossible. We were wondering what we could do to get the flood out of the trench when we saw two or three Jerries climb onto the parapet of their trench and start digging with those long handled shovels of theirs. They must have seen us because as the water came pouring out of their trench, one of them lifted the blade of his shovel into the air and waved a 'washout'. I at once gave them the same signal with the butt of my rifle. It seemed to me that this was an event that was apart from the ordeal and enmity of battle. The forces of nature had restored the sense of common humanity after all the carnage there had been since the battle started. Not a shot was fired on either side while we stood in danger of being drowned.

For the Durham Pals their current purgatory was nearly at an end, as a company of the Gloucesters came up as their relief, 'splashing towards us, I was surprised to see that they were in khaki shorts'. Charles Moss and his gunners plodged back along Eczema trench, away from the front line: 'It was nearly dark when we got out of the communication trench. Here we found a great dump where troops from other regiments who had been relieved were dumping fighting equipment they had salvaged from the battlefield. We had to leave on this dump the Lewis gun that we'd picked up. But when the gun we carried back to battalion was checked the next day, it was found, by its number, which we had not been able to check in the dark, that we had left our gun on the dump and brought back the one we'd found. This incident gave me further proof of the callousness and inflexibility of army routine and discipline. We had survived five days and nights of exhausting experiences but these stood for nothing in comparison to having brought the wrong gun back to Battalion!'

Despite the suffering and horrors of their tour in the trenches, Charles Moss and his Pals had not quailed in their terrible ordeal. Their baptism on the Western Front had been both harrowing and relentless. Yet these were not regular soldiers, they were a citizen army:

Our feelings had not been brutalised by our civilian occupations, we were not time-serving professional soldiers. Most of us had left soft jobs. We had in the ranks many with college and university educations, who had volunteered for the duration of the war. When our battalion had been formed we had not been psychologically hardened for the hardship and mentality of the rank and file regulars … I was deeply thankful to be able to answer the roll-call that so many thousands would fail to do after the first phase of the many phases of the criminal waste of men and material in the Battle of the Somme.

The year 1916 drew to a close with both the Allies and Germans pretty much where they'd been at the start. Two great battles, dwarfing in scale those which had gone earlier, had demanded a vast blood sacrifice. Neither side was seemingly any nearer to breaking the deadlock.

CHAPTER 4

MUD

1917

For Sir Douglas Haig, 1917 would not prove to be a vintage year. His early offensive at Arras and Vimy achieved wonders at the outset, though the former swiftly degenerated into costly attrition. General Plumer and the Second Army performed tremendous feats at Messines. But then Haig's great summer offensive, the third battle of Ypres, popularly better known by the name of one of its objectives, Passchendaele, became the very symbol of fruitless slaughter in a hellish sea of mud.

Arras and Messines

On 9 April, Haig attacked at Arras. This was essentially a large-scale diversion intended to keep German reserves pinned in that sector whilst General Nivelle's master plan unfolded. On the first day the Canadian Corps, fighting as a single cohesive force for the first time, performed magnificently and took Vimy Ridge. This seemingly impregnable bastion had bloodily defied all Allied attempts for the preceding three years. Allenby's Third Army made astonishing progress on the first day at Arras. Despite the vastly improved bombardment and deep penetrations the

British could not capitalise on this initial success. The Germans, resilient as ever, recovered their breath and stood their ground. The battle went grinding on, the same weary and bloody toll of attrition; Allenby losing over four thousand men a day till further attacks were finally called off on 17 May.

Sir Douglas Haig had plans for that approaching summer. He was always of the belief that Flanders was the crucial sector and that it was here the war would be lost and won. His plan for 1917 was an ambitious one. He proposed that a major thrust would secure the higher ground that was crowned by the small town of Passchendaele whilst a strong left hook would punch a path clear towards the Channel ports which could be seized in a coordinated amphibious operation. This was bold indeed and flew in the face of more conservative, purely military concepts of 'bite and hold'. Haig's task was an unenviable one for whatever he proposed had to pass a hostile war cabinet and thus he had to dangle the carrot of great gains – almost certainly unattainable.

Before this great offensive could be launched, vital high ground around Messines and Wytschaete, ceded in 1914, had to be won back, a mission entrusted to 'Daddy' Plumer. This was indeed a herculean task but the commander of the Second Army was ready. His 30,000 tunnellers had been digging beneath German lines since 1915. Mining was an area where the British had built up vast expertise and a clear superiority. Plumer's preparations were meticulous.

Logistics and intensive training were undertaken methodically and efficiently. Artillery preparation was far more sophisticated and effective than in the previous year. At 03.10 on the morning of 7 June, 19 great mines exploded beneath Messines Ridge, eruptions of biblical and apocalyptic proportions, which jellified stunned survivors. By Great War standards the battle was a resounding success with moderate losses, an impressive bag of enemy dead and some 7,000 prisoners.

Captain John Evelyn Carr, destined for a role in this offensive, was serving with 11th Battalion, Sherwood Foresters in Flanders in the early part of 1917:

> On Easter Monday which was somewhere near the end of March the Germans made a very determined attack on that portion of the line, held by 11th Sherwood Foresters. They came over very suddenly in large numbers, in the early morning just before daylight; they got through our front line and there were heavy casualties on both sides. Some of the Boche got right down to our Battalion HQ. Amongst others who were killed was our adjutant Lieutenant Cavell who was a cousin of Nurse Cavell who was murdered in Brussels. He met the Boche face to face and was shot at arm's length, a good many of the HQ personnel were also killed with another officer named Thorn. The Germans all carried dozens of egg bombs and had picks and shovels with them, so they'd evidently intended to stay. They were all driven out; either killed or wounded but the operation cost us between 40–50 men and three officers.

By late April, he was assigned in a training role, based at Toronto Camp, and in early May, the drums could clearly be heard, their

Captain Oliver Woodward was a Queensland miner who earned the Military Cross for his service with the 1st Australian Tunnelling Company, a battalion of miners and engineers recruited to tunnel silently under the German lines. Their mission was to detonate a massive store of explosives 30 metres underground and plunge the German troops in the trenches above into chaos. At 03.10 on 7 June 1917, their work culminated in what was then the largest man-made explosion in history as a series of 19 underground bombs, totalling 450,000 kg of high explosives were detonated in a mighty eruption that was reportedly felt in London, 200 kilometres away.

tempo building: 'We have come to this area so the brigade can practice for the attack we are to make at the beginning of June. Trenches have all been prepared as near as possible to the German lines we shall have to take which are on Wytschaete Ridge, near Messines.' Carr was, by this time, attached to Battalion HQ: 'We were kept very busy and had to do most of our work between six and ten in the morning so the ground would be fully ready. In this village [Boeschepe] cock fighting is carried on and we got to two or three fights while we were here.' He returned to the line 22/23 May, now as CO of 'Halifax' training camp:

It is not very far from Vlamertinghe, the camp was a little distant from my billet and my mess was inside the camp in a hut. On 24th May, Goldman (gas officer) and I went up to Poperinghe for dinner at Skindles. In the middle of dinner the town was bombarded and there was a great panic. One shell hit the building we were in, glass and brick were hurled onto our plates. The waiters quite simply flew down to the cellar and left us all to help ourselves and we did so, especially with the wine! There was a great amount of damage done in Poperinghe and on our way home we noticed one house, the front of which had been ripped clean off and the house opened up from top to bottom with everything, furniture, bedding etc intact. In the dusk and walking along dusty roads we passed long, long lines of transport; a most wonderful sight, miles and miles of men, mules, lorries and carts.

By 26 May, the drums were sounding louder still: 'Our camps were rather badly shelled this afternoon so we dug some trenches for the men to get into when we are bombarded and thereby saved a good many lives. A band from one of the Welsh regiments was playing in our camp during the afternoon. What an extraordinary contrast when a band plays "Come to my garden of Roses" accompanied by the thundering of the guns! Both camps and dumps were badly hit, 7th Division's beautiful theatre was absolutely blown away and they lost everything, together with the canteen, YMCA hut and other timber buildings.'

On 5 June the brigade went up into the line: 'The huge mine at Hill 60 at which miners have been working for the last year or two is to be blown up at 3 a.m. on the 7th. I shall not forget that march. It is a sad sort of feeling for all. The band played 'Tipperary' and many other well known tunes, the men were joking all the way along and I felt quite out of it having to come back. Now and then we had a shell near us as we went up. Darkness fell and the voices faded away, the men seemed to have been swallowed up!' The night of 6/7 June was electric. Everyone knew the offensive was due to unfold and that the mines would explode first:

> Captain Payne came along to our bivouac and we sat with our watches on the table. The time for Hill 60 to go was 3.30 a.m. ten minutes before; we filled up our glasses and waited. The time came and, almost to the second, there was a rumbling noise and the whole world seemed to shake. I could see the whisky and water in our glasses quivering for some time but there was no huge report. Mr. Lloyd George at Walton Heath who said he heard the report must have had his nerves worked up to some pitch as it was a dead sort of noise and how we knew it had gone was by the shaking ground but the noise from the guns after that moment was fearsome and deafening.

On 7 June the assaults drove forward, British gains were impressive and optimism prevailed.

> We had a very large haul of prisoners during the day. I cannot remember how many, a curious crowd including many officers who were very surly and resented being examined. The men were very dirty, haggard, hungry and thirsty looking creatures. Some were terrible looking creatures, Russians who the Germans had made fight for them. As soon as they got out of sight of their officers, they became different men and appeared to be very glad to be caught and their spirits rise the further away from the shelling of their own guns they get. Generally, the news was very good and things had gone almost better than we had expected, we'd got well onto Messines Ridge.

Despite the success at Messines, there was no immediate follow-up and Crown Prince Rupprecht of Bavaria, commanding German forces in Flanders, was given time to take in the lessons of Messines and strengthen his line accordingly. He was advised by Colonel Fritz von Lossberg, the Vauban of trench warfare. He now created a series of grid fortifications studded with redoubts and fronted by a deep but thinly held outpost line, manned primarily by machine gunners sheltering in blockhouses or ruined farms. These, the elite of the German army, promised to exact a high toll of any attacker before the main line was ever reached.

Third Ypres – the first attacks

Haig was partly hamstrung by political doubts. The war cabinet was insisting on adequate French support for his main offensive. In the circumstances, this appeared highly improbable. It was not until 25 July that he was given the green light. The intervening weeks had given Rupprecht the breathing space he needed and Flanders weather was clearly with him: generations of patient farmers had corralled the waters in the area by ingenious irrigation and drainage but three years of neglect and endless churning of shells had destroyed their clever systems. The summer of 1917 was exceptionally wet. Mud was the prevailing characteristic of Flanders that year.

Arthur William David Roberts was a mixed-race soldier born in Bristol in 1897. His father, David, was a ship's steward who married a Bristol woman. At some point in the early 20th century the family moved to Glasgow where the young Arthur remained in full-time education till he was 18. It is clear from the quality of his prose he was a highly intelligent and articulate young man, something of a 'dandy' in his style. For most of his adult, working life Arthur was employed as a marine engineer but he volunteered for military service in 1917, firstly with the 2nd Battalion, KOSB, and latterly 2nd Battalion, Royal Scottish Fusiliers:

For so short an army career, I think I may safely say, my life during that period was as varied, and eventful, as most private soldiers of a similar length of service. A soldier during war time if capable is pushed into many breaches whether fit for the front line or base. I have been fit for both; consequently I have filled many breaches. The last sentence will perhaps lead the reader to think I am possessed of great capabilities, and this belief may be strengthened when I say that I have been company-runner, batman, guide, dining-hall attendant, bugler, dispatch clerk, aircraft-gunner, hut-builder, stretcher-bearer, and one or two other things. Now it has been unintentional, if I have seemingly blown my own horn about my military accomplishments, but I think this book, written as frankly as I could write it will exonerate me from any imputation of self-aggrandizement.

His first experience of the trenches was in the spring of 1917, as the BEF was gearing up for the third battle of Ypres: 'I first actually entered the trenches on the dawn of 9th June, 1917. I can tell you, after our gruelling march, I was a physical wreck. That night as I plumped down in a dugout, I was so tired that without taking off my equipment, I almost immediately fell into a trance. All the Kaiser's horses and all the Kaiser's men could not have put the wind up me that night.' Even sentry duty was, in the first undreamed of instance, a novelty:

Of course it was novel to me so the time did not seem so long as it did later on. When the novelty wears off it is a dreary, monotonous watch and at this time of the year in France, the early mornings are very cold and usually wet. At times like these, a chap often imagines he sees things such as men crawling about in front and when the wind blows stray whispers of barbed wire against the metal poles it confirms the idea. Often a chap with this belief will open fire and consequently the parapet is manned at once and everybody has a go at something imaginary. Naturally, Gerry gets the wind up and he starts rifles, machine-guns, and bombs, grenades and the racket might last about an hour then fizzle out. Next day's news; a strong attack on our trenches was successfully beaten off, many casualties to enemy.

Prior to the opening attacks, which would be directed at recovering ground at Pilckem Ridge, Gheluvelt and Langemarck, gunners of Plumer's Second Army and Gough's Fifth pumped over 4,500,000 shells into von Lossberg's improved defences. The toll of German defenders was terrible and damage, not just to defences, but to the quaking ground, considerable. On 31 July, British infantry went over the top in Flanders.

For Arthur Roberts, like so many tens of thousands of other Tommies, the opening of Haig's great summer offensive and the battles which followed proved their baptism and Calvary combined: 'It was the 29th July 1917 and we were lying on the outskirts of Dickebusch waiting to move up to go over the top … The ground, being low lying, soon became a mass of mud and slime, the small bivouac tents were poor shelters from the drenching downpour. Under such conditions no fires could possibly be lit. All that day we squatted under our low tents, wet and miserable, so that when orders came to prepare to move we were glad to have something to do.' Their march was purgatory:

At the appointed time we 'fell in' and muddy and weary as we were, we started forward, with the slow, ponderous movement so common to the BEF. The roads were calf deep with mud, while the rest of the country was half-lake, half quagmire. Frequently, enemy shells would land in the near vicinity with sudden slaps and mud showers, so that we had a mud bath every now and then. Dead animals and disabled wagons lay scattered in profusion. In many cases, these objects were almost buried in the boggy terrain. At last we came to a corduroy road that is a roadway of tree trunks which was also plentifully dotted with deceased mules and timber wagons. This road was the stopping point for the transport evidently and some of them had stopped for good. We turned along this road and slipping and stumbling over the wet logs, we made our way cursing and grousing until we came upon our own transport wagons, waiting to be unloaded.

Finally, they plodded into the shallow communication trench: 'The sides of the trench were of such shifting nature that frames

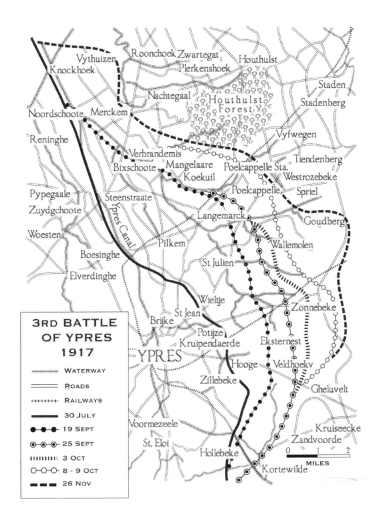

3RD BATTLE OF YPRES 1917

~~	WATERWAY
═══════	ROADS
┼┼┼┼┼┼┼	RAILWAYS
━━━━━━	30 JULY
●─●─●	19 SEPT
◉─◉─◉	25 SEPT
∥∥∥∥∥∥	3 OCT
○─○─○	8 - 9 OCT
▬ ▬ ▬	26 NOV

of wire netting were required to hold them up. The least touch caused slime to ooze through. The bottom was on average covered by a foot of water; plainly speaking what was being misnamed as a trench, was only a common ditch. In the dry season I should say it would be about six feet deep, at this time it was anything from seven feet.' Arthur selected the driest funk hole he could find but, barely had he laid aside his rifle than he and several others found themselves selected for fatigues. In this case it was the laborious business of unloading transport wagons. An old hand by now; 'ah well, I thought now I'm here I'll make the best of it and I selected a sack of jam. These needed less careful handling and all true soldiers always keep an eye for the main chance. Before I regained the ditch, one of the pots of jam was mine!'

That night, they stood or huddled in their sludge-garnished ditch, damp creeping through muscle and bone, no bright explosion of summer dawn, just a dank, cloying mist. All day they remained in uncomfortable waiting, 'like kittens in a box we became restless as the day advanced'. Their trumpet to glory did not sound that day, however and, 'darkness again closed down upon us, bringing fresh supplies of rain and we longed for the attack if only to relieve our monotony. The water in our ditch had risen considerably, but we thought it better to stand in it than out on top getting the icy wind that was blowing.' At 21.00 the rum ration arrived with orders for movement at midnight. Arthur was not a drinking man 'but this night I would have supped with the devil himself if I could have bettered my case by doing so. Rum rations at the best were never of generous proportions ... but as we were all fairly well knocked up, the ration on this occasion was passable. Mine, I know, did wonders for me.'

They marched under the wet blanket of darkness 'moving along the intricate trenches like a giant reptile wriggling through an enormous crooked tube'. Each by now had acquired an outer casing of Flanders mud, 'but I have to admit even if it is dirty it certainly keeps the heat in and the cold out'. Their laborious, slime-drenched marches were drawing them closer to the front:

> German artillery kept up a desultory action but he was registering too close for our comfort. As we proceeded the effects of the gunfire were becoming more apparent to us. The trenches were taking on a more battered look and the dead men lying in them were getting

more numerous as we went forward. The trenches had been so badly shelled that in some places we were walking in the open, where big shell holes had taken the place of that bit of trench. In the surviving lengths, dead men were so numerous it was impossible proceed without walking on them. This section of trenches was awful. One moment we were wading up to our middles in water, the next we were wobbling and balancing over the bodies of our unfortunate comrades.

… that journey was like a nightmare, even yet as I write this I can fancy I can see the gruesome forms lying in the flooded craters by the green relief of Verey lights which reflected on the ink-black water, casting an opalescent glow on the ghastly faces. There was no time, nor was this the place to be sentimental and we were hurried forward to be in our positions by 2 a.m., the appointed time for the kick-off.

Soon it would be their turn: 'As we knelt there, waiting the command of our officer who constantly gazed at his wrist watch with the sheet of blackness before us, and the German curtain-fire behind us, roaring in its seeming impatience; my thoughts were strangely far distant from the battlefield.' Arthur was swept with a wave of pure pride, 'here I was among men sharing the risks and uncertainties of being in the very front ranks of the Empire against its enemies; patriotism was strong in my breast then.' Reality, 'the tiny grim imp' swiftly re-asserted itself; 'waiting is worse than a hundred deaths – Heavens, will the order never come. Whizz! Shhh! Crash! Bang! Boom! 'Forward men', calmly said our officer.' His fears of fear forgot in the rush of action, Arthur with his comrades struggled ahead into no man's land:

The barrage of our guns fell about fifty yards ahead, exactly at 2 a.m., for a few minutes it shattered and battered the German front line, and then it roared forward. It was as if the earth had opened in half and vomited forth flames and sparks of gorgeous rich colours.

The ground was in an awful miry state, but we had not squelched forward very far before three or four prisoners came up to us unarmed and with hands held high. Our officer obtained what information he could but the corporal treated them guardedly as if they had been bristling with guns. We had no time to lose, so we hurried on as best we could but with the boggy ground and detours we had to make round small lakes, our barrage soon thundered away into the distance, leaving us hopelessly behind. The section about thirty yards on our right, received a heavy German shell right in their midst. Shortly afterwards, I saw one of the tanks in front of us catch fire. I think by the blaze it must have been a supply tank.

Enemy fire began to take effect: 'the enemy pestered us with a slow but annoying fire of 5.9 shells and an assortment of smaller rounds. As we plunged on, one of our section who was walking at my left shoulder, suddenly collapsed with a sigh, a splinter had pierced his abdomen. Some stretcher bearers were following our party but, before they came up, the poor chap had expired. Afterwards, it was remarked that, during the previous day, the unfortunate man had been very reticent in his speech and actions.' Dawn had overtaken night and the black, mud-slicked plain was deepening in yet more rain, waterlogged shell-holes coalescing into wider lakes of sulphurous filth, 'through which rising pieces of mud appeared like tiny islands'.

Their attack had been carefully rehearsed but the neat topography of a model battlefield and the surgical view of aerial observers did not coincide with the shot-torn morass through which Arthur and his comrades struggled:

> The HQ staff seemed to think the plan would work so, as a consequence, we started off in one direction, then we suddenly swung sharply to the right, then some yards further on, we turned half-left and I'm sure we covered a mile before we even saw a trench. At last we dropped into one and the first thing I saw was an officer lying dead with a handkerchief over his face, and his servant collecting his books and papers.
>
> Now we were in the enemy trenches, our work commenced. We had carried our sacks of bombs a long way, and they were heavy, so we thought the sooner we delivered them, the sooner we would lighten our load. The dead officer made us more merciless than we would otherwise have been, so we went along that trench and every

dugout we came to, we flung in a bomb or two then called on the occupants to come out. The Mills Bomb goes off five seconds after the pin strikes the cap, we held it for three seconds while by the time we had shouted, four seconds had elapsed so that the Jerry down below usually stayed there.

Once again the Tommies were entering a 'race for the parapet'. Their painful and exhausting trek through water and mud meant the creeping barrage sailed off with majestic élan and, 'we were now exposed to the German machine-gunners. Under their withering fire our section was soon dispersed. We would be ploughing forward when suddenly the stutter of a machine-gun and the vicious swish of bullets would send us rolling into the nearest shell-hole, invariably full of water. In a short time officers were without men and men without officers. Bombers and grenadiers and Lewis Gunners and riflemen were all mixed up. Some parties consisted of nearly all NCO's whilst other groups didn't have one. Nevertheless, forwards was the order of the day and mixed up as we were, in parties of threes and fours and in some cases a dozen, we moved on, always being broken up by the gunners. Sometimes, I was alone when a sudden dive for safety would land me among a party.'

Despite the weight of enemy fire and dreadful ground, the attackers slogged forwards: 'Due credit must come in and will be given by me to the German rearguard that held us up that day. It was certain death for them because our waves of infantry had got between them and their main body in most cases. To expose themselves was to draw fire. Like the heroes they were, they fought like tigers, withdrawing from crater to crater and we steadily but very slowly pushed on.' Though the assault progressed, all cohesion had been lost. 'At length I found myself going forward with a lance-corporal and two privates of my own battalion, and a couple of chaps from a Manchester Battalion. We could see none of our own troops near us now and, as we happened on a German trench that was wicker-lined and had at least a semblance of dryness, we dropped in and prepared to hold on till such time as we could reconnect ourselves with another body of our comrades.'

Gunmetal skies continued to spill torrents of rain while tendrils of mist still clung to the fire-gouged field, 'but the stutter of Lewis and machine-guns came to our ears. Occasional bursts of rifle fire now plain, now faint reached us also. The artillery of both sides seemed to have given up the contest. As I peeped over the enemy's parados (the rear of the trench), all I could see were big sheets of water reflecting sullen skies, all lashed by heavy rain while here and there lay a body soaked and sodden and muddy.' During the long day, Arthur and his new comrades held on in their improvised defences. The battlefield now seemed deserted, as though dragged down by the weight of mud and rain. As dusk began to gather, they were relieved, stumbling back to the rally point and a shivering night in dripping woods.

Another wet dawn brought fresh tribulation: 'Parties were told off to act as stretcher-bearers. The party I was with was to carry wounded from a subterranean post to some ruins called Dormie House. The post was a fair distance from the house and it was no joke wading knee deep in mud with one corner of a stretcher on your shoulder. Some German guns were playing on our quarter, and the job was made perfectly nerve-breaking.' For the Scots, already exhausted, begrimed and hungry, the German bombardment proved a particular trial: 'One of our guns had been put out of action near the house and I think Gerry was firing at it, not knowing of its plight. There was mud on nearly every square inch of me. The last issue of rations I had received had been three days before at Zillebeke Lake, since then my iron rations and that purloined pot of jam had been my only subsistence.'

Separated from his fellow stretcher-bearers, Arthur became lost in a fug of exhaustion till, mainly by good luck, he stumbled back into the RAP at Dormie House: 'The RAMC men manning this post and who had been smelling the rum jar oftener than was wise for them, informed me that all the working parties had departed for the night.' Wearily, he departed towards a distant rest: 'Along the masses of communication trenches I plodded, a lonely soul in a lonely landscape. It was still raining. At length I left the trenches, but arriving at our own camp found it deserted. Judge the depths of misery into which I was again cast, I was tired, footsore, weary, hungry and mucky. It was darkening and nobody was in sight.' Despite his numbing tiredness, Arthur spent a fruitless night stumbling through the ravaged land, seeking his battalion. Morning, another rain-swept dawn, brought solace:

> I remember walking towards a cluster of tents and limber wagons. The next thing I recall, I was half-lying against a wagon with rain beating on my face and my own section-officer giving me a good drink of rum. Everybody was pleased to see me but I took most to the post-corporal for he had a parcel and letter for me. I demolished the parcel, the letter had to wait for, like a pig that has been fed, I rolled over and my thick coating of mud helped to keep me warm while I slept.

In the early fighting gains were made, though these were modest when measured against losses. Over such dreadful ground, tanks were of little value, constantly getting bogged down and offering target practice for German gunners. Attacks continued through August though the ghastly weather continued. Von Lossberg's defences proved a very tough nut indeed and, by the end of August, the Fifth Army had lost some 60,000 men.

Third Ypres – the dogfight; Menin Road, Polygon Wood and Broodseinde

When the burden was shifted from the Fifth to the Second Army, Plumer was to focus on the Gheluvelt Plateau. As at Messines, 'Daddy' Plumer had thought long and hard about the tactical problem. His artillery would be both sledgehammer and scalpel whilst still providing a shield to the infantry. Their main assault would be preceded by trained skirmishers, the basis of infiltration tactics. Attacks would proceed on a local 'bite and hold' basis, a pause between each bound for consolidation and allowing fresh units to pass through. Reserves would always be on hand to reinforce success.

Norman Gladden had left school in 1913 intending to join the civil service. He had no notions of going to war – 'fit enough but not robust'. When his call-up papers arrived in May 1916, he was three months short of his 19th birthday. That wash of patriotic fervour that had guided Kitchener's volunteers had receded in the face of a mounting, seemingly never-ending recital of casualties. By now there was no glory, only stalemate. Norman Gladden was initially assigned to the 2nd (Home Service) Battalion of the Hertfordshire Regiment, before he was transferred to 11th Battalion of the Northumberland Fusiliers.

On 31 July, the great offensive in Flanders opened. Private Gladden, whilst on the march, 'saw a detachment of the new Chinese Labour Corps, about the employment of which there had been a good deal of controversy at home. They were hard at work unloading trucks and one might well wonder what was going through their minds at finding themselves thus occupied in a land so far from home.' Billeted in the pleasant village of Quelves, the Northumbrians initially endured no greater discomforts than sharing their barn accommodation with resident livestock and slopping through omnipresent mud.

Few doubted that this was anything other than the calm before the storm: 'Unsettling rumours began to stalk among us, most prominently upon the lips of a corporal who could not resist letting it be known that he was the recipient of "confidential information". The aims of our recent exertions were made plain, if we had been so obtuse as not to have guessed!' As wet August passed into dank September the Northumbrians made ready but no orders came. Billeted now in the hamlet of La Clytte where, 'about the village there were still vestiges of the trench system of 1915 which had linked up with Locre and Kemmel while a small cemetery near the shell-marked church contained the graves of those who fell in the early fighting, honoured warriors of a very different type of warfare.'

By degrees the battalion moved nearer the front, first to Brewery Camp by Dickebusch, dwelling in sandbagged bell tents: 'most of [the camp's] recent occupants had been shelled out of the place, a report that was supported by the existence in the vicinity of a number of large shell craters.' Gladden was part of a Lewis gun team and improvised timber mounts for anti-aircraft fire had been rigged up:

> We had not long to wait. Across the skies, sailing obliquely towards the camp, a regular enemy armada of planes was approaching, large bombing machines flanked by numbers of lighter scout planes. As they passed unhurriedly above, I counted at least fifteen large aircraft. Men crammed the shallow drainage gutters which criss-crossed between the lines or bunched down behind the low sandbag barriers by the tents.
>
> The three of us remaining near the gun with spare ammunition ready, stood up like magnified targets before the approaching enemy. Goffee [Lewis gunner] fired up towards the advance line which was probably flying much too high for us to reach while the number one and I crouched nearby. Shrapnel and bullets splattered around. The marauders were directly overhead still sailing forward with majestic unconcern. I felt a catch in my breath and my heart seemed to stand still but no bombs fell and for us at least the danger had passed.

Other camps nearby were not spared.

As the vortex of battle inexorably sucked fresh blood into its maw the Northumbrians moved up to the support line. Bouts of offensive were interspersed with preparation, livened by raids: 'I was filled with great admiration for these volunteers. Among them, I remember one man in particular, a private who acted as one of our company runners. Unmilitary in appearance and small of stature, always undemonstrative under stress; he neither gained any distinction nor accepted any rank.'

The Fusiliers moved through the tortured skeleton of Ypres, past Shrapnel Corner, moving over the shell-scarred waste along an elevated timber causeway:

> Eventually we approached the ridge where the scene of desolation challenged description. All around us stretched a morass in shades of grey and black, looking like some petrified inferno from Dante. Waterlogged shell-holes almost touched one another, rendering the ground pretty near impassable except where the duckboards ran. Gaunt, leafless trees stood out aimlessly here and there to break the monotony. Perched along the ridge itself one of our field batteries was firing furiously over the barrier while heavy German shells were searching along the crest in reply. In the hollow lay the derelict corpses of a couple of tanks, hopelessly bogged and badly shattered.

Zero hour on 20 September was set for 05.40 and the battalions were to be ready in their jumping-off trenches by 03.30. Once the barrage lifted, 11th RNF would attack and take the Red Line, allowing their comrades in 10th Battalion to pass through and assault the further, Blue Line:

> An officer, coming forward from the groups behind us, snapped his watch into his pocket and signalled us forward. We were moving; a few moments' silence – intensified; eternal! Then the guns crashed out from behind us and we were running forward in the reflected

Sandbags have been in use since the 18th century, with the earliest used recorded by British Loyalists under siege during the American War of Independence. Empty burlap bags were easy to transport and could be filled by shovel when needed. Extreme care was needed when stacking them as they could collapse inwards, especially if filled with local clay rather than sand.

light of the artillery. I could feel and see crowds of men moving on all sides, spreading waves of humanity, directing their puny flesh toward the enemy positions. The earth simply shook with the discharge. The air above us seemed to be roofed with rushing shells, whilst some way ahead a curtain of flame and smoke completely blotted out the landscape.

Now, I experienced a peculiar almost dreamlike emotion. Though my feet were moving with all the energy needed to carry me with my burden across the ground, I felt that they were in fact rooted to the earth and that it was all my surroundings that were moving of their own accord. Our barrage; a wave of inconceivable confusion, began to creep away from the edge of the wood, whose trees stood out ever more clearly as the fumes gradually cleared. Now, the whole situation changed as if by magic, evil magic for us! Zipping sniper's bullets began their deadly work. Machine-guns opening out ahead began to traverse methodically across our front like flails of death, crossing and re-crossing as they sprayed the advancing lines. I felt the tearing stream of lead swishing across as the muzzles elevated and could scarcely believe I had not been hit.

A man a few yards ahead slipped to the ground and lay in a heap. Sergeant Rhodes was still in front, urging the men forward. Machine-guns cut across again and single rifle shots syncopated their steadier rattle. The defenders were resisting with deadly effect. I heard screams around me. Agony and death seemed to be cutting into the advancing lines. From the edge of the wood, now much closer, flashes from rifles and machine-guns filled the air like venomous darts.

I could distinguish our front wave clearly for daylight was fully upon us and if I had further capacity for fear such fear gripped me now. Men in front were dropping to earth, whether from wounds or for cover I could not know.

By now 'B' Company coming up behind were bunching with the survivors of 'A'. Norman Gladden took advantage of a scrape in the ravaged earth to seek sanctuary from a merciless fire. Attempts to dig in were futile. One comrade who whipped out his entrenching tool immediately had the handle shattered by a random shot; 'a sniper clearly had the spot marked'. Dead and wounded crumpled in and around, 'in my imagination, the pincers of death were closing in upon this spot for my insignificant benefit'. This hiatus was short-lived:

> There had been a halt in the forward flow which now resumed with increasing momentum. My inaction now became intolerable. I gathered myself to rise and dash forward, hoping that the sniper had been dislodged or had better marks for his rifle. Our barrage was well forward, no longer followed by masses of troops. The attackers were moving all over the place in scattered groups, taking advantage of any cover they could find. Wicked 5.9 bursts were churning up the ground behind me … straight ahead there was a gradual slope to the low horizon, practically free of moving men.

Like a parting of the waves, the impetus of attack slewed away from the open rise, either towards the woods to the left or towards an enemy parapet on the right. For Norman Gladden, as the trench seemed nearer, it offered the less risky alternative. 'I reached the trench and, as I breasted the parapet of the German defensive position, my eyes fell upon a site of horrible carnage. A splutter of bullets forced me down amidst the horror. The trench, which was little more than a wide gash in the ground, was strewn with dead and dying, British and Germans in grim equality.'

Objective reports might consider the situation fluid. In fact it was a shambles of confusion. The plan was that 10th RNF and 13th DLI would pass through to assault both the Blue and Green lines. Norman Gladden, crouched in the temporary, blood-washed haven of the German trench could not see any of his comrades from 11th NF. To regain the survivors of the unit he would have to attempt the perilous dash over open ground to the fringe of the woods. 'Running across from shell-hole to shell-hole, I eventually struck the woods diagonally some way in advance and was pleased to join a party of troops who had collected near an enemy strongpoint.'

All of the company officers were down, dead or wounded. Redoubtable Sergeant Rhodes now commanded the remnants:

Within the shifting carapace of trees, groups filtered blindly. All order and cohesion had gone. For a while Gladden was put in charge of a small group of British wounded, a task he hardly relished. Despite his own terrors, he was aware he still packed the spare drums for the Lewis gun. These would be needed. He had to press on, beyond the wood where Tower Hamlets Ridge swelled just ahead. In this flat, sodden polder even the suggestion of higher ground counted: 'In the foreground, a little to my left, there was a hollow which contained two greenish, muddy patches. These had been, as I was later to discover, ornamental ponds in a park which were marked on the map as Dumbarton Lakes. One was still crossed by the damaged timbers of a rustic bridge and, on the far side; men were digging.'

He had found the survivors of his own platoon, still led by Sergeant Rhodes and was re-united with his comrades from the Lewis gun team. Casualties had been heavy but the tide of battle had moved forwards over Tower Hamlets Ridge. Nonetheless, German snipers were still a regular menace:

Wristwatches had been around for a while but were regarded as a bit *effete* (although some officers had used them during the Second Boer War), and an officer with his pocket watch was a typical sight in the early part of the war. The creeping barrage artillery tactic, developed during the war, required precise synchronisation between the artillery gunners and advancing infantry requiring shared timepieces. Service watches produced during the war were specially designed for the rigours of trench warfare, with luminous dials and unbreakable glass. Wristwatches were also found to be needed in the air as much as on the ground. The British War Department began issuing them from 1917.

The Souvenir King, Private John Hines of the Australian 45th Battalion surrounded by German equipment he looted during the battle of Polygon Wood in September 1917. (Frank Hurley, Australian War Memorial, via Wikimedia Commons)

We both admired and hated these brave men. Admired them for their persistence and bravery, hated them, illogically to some extent for what we considered was unsportsmanlike action. Possibly they were more desperate than brave, having been taught that they would get no quarter in any case. Of course, their persistence meant that it often worked out this way, for the moppers up would have been foolish to take any chances.

It wasn't until midnight on 21 September that survivors of 'A' Company, having seen off several enemy counter-attacks, were withdrawn.

In Staff College terms, the attacks on 20 September were successful. Attacking formations, moving behind the barrage, attained their objectives. Swift consolidation meant ruin for the three German divisions sent into counter-attack. 'Daddy' Plumer's careful and considered preparations had again paid dividends. On 26 September, Plumer once more attacked and

Tyne Cot Cemetery marks the final line of attack up the deceptively shallow ridge. The cemetery acquired its name from the Northumberland Fusiliers, who thought the German concrete blockhouses on the site resembled Tyneside miners' cottages. With nearly 12,000 burials it is the largest Commonwealth War Graves Commission burial ground in the world. Designed by Sir Herbert Baker, the panels on the rear wall of the cemetery commemorate some 35,000 men who fell in the salient after 15 August 1917 and who have no known grave.

the Australians took Polygon Wood. His third bound on 3 October came up against modified German response tactics and the Anzacs had to use their bayonets in taking Windmill Hill.

On 26 October the Canadians began their assault on the pulverised ruins of Passchendaele. On 6 November, they took the place. Fighting stuttered on for another couple of weeks till late autumn finally closed in on the battlefield. British casualties were stated as 244,897 dead, wounded and missing, German losses were estimated as considerably higher. Not everyone accepted this and the political consensus appears to have been that losses were about equal at nearly 400,000 each. There had been no breakthrough.

CHAPTER 5

BREAKTHROUGH

1918

Who was the wag, who during a weary march in file from the ramparts to the trenches, passed back the message; 'Last man shut the Menin Gate?'

The Kaiser's battle

GEORGE HARBOTTLE WAS, AT THE WAR'S outset, apprenticed to Tyneside shipbrokers Cairns Noble, based on the bustling quayside. George and his best pal Laurie Benson joined the flood, enlisting in 6th Battalion, Northumberland Fusiliers:

> Having reported to 'A' Company at Tilley's I was somewhat saddened to find we were all ensconced on the beautiful dance hall floor on whose surface I had spent many a delightful evening in very different company from the heavy, army booted denizens with their dixies of tea or stew slopping about on that sacred floor.

George spent two years in the infantry, seeing much action. In 1916 he retrained with the newly formed Machine Gun Corps, commissioned into the 15th Battalion. An MGC battalion comprised 'four companies commanded by a major with a captain as 2I/C. each company had 16 guns 'arranged in four sections of four guns'. In the divisional structure, each MG company worked with a brigade. This was not a popular arrangement as the MG officers ruled their own fiefs and were not directly answerable to the infantry. In March 1917 George found himself at Arras, 'the front was a strong one, because we had gained the best strategic positions in our successful offensive in Easter 1917'.

For George Harbottle, his comrades in 15th Battalion, MGC, and for the whole of the BEF, an immense trial now lay ahead. By early 1918, fully fledged German storm battalions, their firepower beefed up with more machine guns, flamethrowers and an infantry gun battery, were being groomed to break the deadlock. Their role was to punch a hole through the defenders' lines, attacking at the weakest spot, then pushing on, leaving the business of mopping up to infantry moving in behind.

General Ludendorff, despite sweeping victories and Russia's near collapse in the east, knew that time was a luxury he did not possess. Russia might be prostrate but America was now entering the war. Though her troops were initially few, the trickle would soon swell into flood. To break the front meant breaking the British, now senior partners in the original alliance. If Germany could successfully break through in the north and turn the Allied flank – as had been attempted in autumn 1914 – the long-delayed victor's laurels might still rest with Kaiser Wilhelm.

For Haig, his opponent's timing could not have been worse. The BEF was ground down by cruel losses in the preceding year. Conscripts dragged unwillingly into the terrible attrition were not the men their bright-eyed predecessors of 1914 or 1916 had been. As the French stumbled, the BEF had to accept responsibility for yet more ground. New responses were needed to shifting German tactics. Lloyd George and his 'Easterners' had little time for their commander-in-chief. His pleas for more men went largely unanswered. Besides, there were no more to be had. Britain and Germany were like two punch-drunk fighters clinging to the canvas, both very nearly played out but unwilling to quit the ring.

British military intelligence was aware the blow must fall. The question was where. To cope with these new threats and reflecting the transitions in positional warfare through 1917, the British line was now a layer cake of three connected levels. A lightly held forward zone relied upon wired-in redoubts, supported by machine guns and a thin artillery line. Perhaps a mile or more behind was the fighting line with most of the infantry and more guns. Behind all this was the rear or support zone. Like most innovations, this revised system had its critics and some local commanders retained a tendency to stuff too many soldiers into the forward zone. Gough had 14 under-strength divisions to hold over 40 miles of the line. His defences were patchy, often incomplete. An invitation to disaster, not one Ludendorff could afford to refuse. George Harbottle was one who witnessed the breaking storm:

> On the morning of Thursday, 21st March, I came out of my dugout with my runner to stand to at dawn with my guns. We were walking along the top of the trench when suddenly there came the biggest bang I have ever heard or ever wish to. The German 1918 offensive had started and at Zero-hour everything had opened up simultaneously. The green, yellow and white SOS lights were shooting up into the air and all our artillery was busy immediately plastering the enemy lines, as were our own machine guns.

George's machine gunners were in the second line, around the village of Monchy le Preux, mostly occupying old German positions, captured in the previous year's savage fighting: 'the place stank like nothing on earth ... a great many horses had been killed there'.

In George's sector the front line, despite a massive bombardment, appeared to be holding. 'What we did not know was that south of us our lines had been completely broken and the enemy was pouring through the gaps he had made on a wide front.' Indeed he was. Fog blanketed the initial German attacks, conferring some respite from British machine-gun fire, and parties of storm-troopers infiltrated behind the forward redoubts. Despite heroic stands such as that of the 16th Manchester Battalion, ground was swiftly lost and in some cases the defence was at best half-hearted. By the end of that first day, Britain had lost 38,000 men, over half of whom were prisoners.

'South of Arras, the German advance went sweeping on and most of the land they had given up when they retired to the Hindenburg line had now been retaken. Even our old trench line system that we had held before our July 1916 Somme offensive was soon to be penetrated'. Amiens and Arras, key bastions, were threatened. It was a very black time for the BEF. George Harbottle and his machine gunners had withdrawn to an old German redoubt in the valley that lies between Tilloy and Monchy le Preux. The place was strong but isolated. George was sent back to the top of the ridge to seek further guidance from the infantry. A further withdrawal into the main Tilloy line was urgently recommended.

'Where the hell are you going?' An engineer officer demanded as he returned down the valley, with uncomfortable news that the

In 1918, Ludendorff introduced **infiltration tactics** to the Western Front. This was a resurrection of the grenadier companies of the 17th and 18th centuries who were used as heavily armed shock troops to attack enemy fortified positions. The German version was battalions of chosen men, well armed with the new sub-machine gun, flamethrowers and light artillery pieces. Their job was to smash through the weak point and keep on going, a footsoldier's *blitzkrieg*.

position had been overrun. There was nothing for it but to pelt back uphill, fearful of what might have become of his company. In fact the machine gunners had wisely withdrawn beforehand; 'I found them in a strong position in our front line on the ridge with a beautiful field of fire over the whole valley.' For the Germans Tilloy Ridge would be a very formidable obstacle. George's guns would have inflicted grievous loss but the swell of attacks ebbed like a receding tide. On one flank, George's division was thrown forward to keep contact northwards. On the other, the line was bent to the right as forces southward were still being pushed back.

At the Doullens conference on 26 March, Allied fears resounded like the clap of doom. Haig was under pressure from Lord Milner and from the newly appointed CIGS Sir Henry Wilson. The upshot was that Foch assumed de facto overall command of all Allied forces – for the first time the Allies would come under a unified command structure. Haig had previously agreed to be subordinate to the bombastic Nivelle, if not with good grace. Here was something different, the makings of a real partnership. Despite the disasters that had befallen the BEF, the British were was still very much in the ring.

For George Harbottle and his gunners, there was little fresh employment. German attacks at Arras had largely petered out: 'Our front was now unusual for trench warfare. Throughout the years we had lived most of our time in two strong trench lines, with barbed wire in front of them and a fairly narrow No-Man's-Land in between. Our present front was much more fluid, with some debatable and some unoccupied places in the valley area between our old front line from Fampoux to Monchy and our present position at Tilloy and Feuchy. One of the most dangerous of these places was up the Scarpe River Valley, which runs from Feuchy through to Fampoux and was still fairly well wooded.' A brace of wily Gordon Highlanders, cut off in the initial onslaught on 21 March, made it back to British lines having survived a vagabond existence in the maze of old trenches and abandoned dugouts.

One of the machine gunners' outposts was both remote and exposed. It could only be relieved at night. 'Rather a difficult place to locate in the darkness because it had to be approached alongside the little Scarpe River … this narrow little valley was littered with half broken trees, branches, undergrowth and rocks and could lead us onto the German lines unless due care was exercised'. When George's section attempted a midnight relief, their guide got hopelessly lost, quailing before the NCO's invective. After some coaxing, he found the way. This position was at the front of the front, hopelessly exposed to shellfire during daylight hours. So, the machine gunners spent their days crouched in a rather makeshift and unsound dugout. They lived like creatures of the night, only surfacing in darkness or, should it come, in the moments before an attack. None did come.

Their next, equally improvised, lodgings were further back, in a warren of passages burrowed into a railway embankment. Here, their existence was little more comfortable, 'the only literature I could muster in my dugout was a month old continental *Daily Mail* and the Horsforth Chapel magazine which had been left behind by a previous occupier. Curiously enough I had often attended that chapel as a boy when visiting an aunt who lived there just outside Leeds.' Ludendorff's offensive was slackening into fresh attrition, the more ground taken, the greater the burden of tenure. On 28 March, he unleashed *Mars* – a fresh blow but like breakers beating on the shore, the hurricane force was fading. On 11 April, Haig issued his famous 'backs to the wall' order but the crisis had already passed.

Next, Ludendorff would try further north where *Georgette* represented a weakened thrust. The more ambitious *George* offensive had earlier been discarded in favour of the onslaught against Gough's Fifth Army:

> The Germans had now dug in round the perimeter of their Amiens Salient early in April and on the 8th had launched a new attack in the Lys River, Armentières area. Part of this front was being held

by the Portuguese contingent (known to our troops as the 'Pork & Beans') and the weight of the onslaught was just too much for them …

The Portuguese were in the line by Neuve Chapelle and *Georgette* inflicted another smashing blow into the British sector. All the gains of 1917 – the terrible, bloody mud-coated slog up Passchendaele Ridge – were lost and Tommies fought to hold the ancient Vauban walls of Ypres itself.

Like their enemies, the Germans were scraping the barrel. Their surviving elite were groomed for the storm-trooper battalions but these paid a heavy price. The rank and file coming on behind often failed to exhibit the iron discipline so expected of the German war machine. 'The German troops were not the highly disciplined quality as in the past and there were many occasions when they got out of hand and started to loot the shops of towns and villages. These places that they had now reached, such as Estaires and Merville, had up to now, been normal places untouched by the war with shops fully stocked …'

George's previous division, the 50th Northumbrian, was amongst those relieved when Foch sent up reinforcements.

Books were much sought after and were a favoured form of comfort from home. In December 1915, *The War Illustrated* published an article about how soldiers found solace from reading and needed books to be sent from Britain. It reveals the men had no appetite for 'literary essays by literary men. What is wanted there is the friendly companionship of a good and kindly book to take the mind away from the contemplation of the terrible environment.' It reveals demand for romance and Jane Austen in particular but little interest in adventure novels.

Re-deployed in a nominally quiet sector between Soissons and Rheims on the line of the Aisne and Aisne Canal, they found their welcome rest very short. This area along the Chemin des Dames, so frequently fought over was now considered 'the sanatorium of the Western Front'. It was over this unsuspecting ground that Ludendorff unleashed *Blucher*, his next attempt. Again, initial gains were made and the Allied defenders, assailed by George "Breakthrough" Bruchmüllers brilliantly directed guns, were pushed back savagely. Then this fresh offensive, like its predecessors, ran out of steam. By this time the Northumbrians had lost heavily. George Harbottle, whose MG company formed part of 15th Scottish Division, found himself being redeployed further south towards the new cauldron north of Amiens.

'Tout le monde à la bataille'

On 3 June the Americans fought their first action at Château-Thierry. Their next and savage baptism occurred in the bloody fight for Belleau Wood where they took all their objectives though at very high cost. It was not until 18 July that Foch launched the first major Allied counter-attack, led by General Mangin's Tenth Army. By the start of August, the initiative had passed fully to the Allies. The Americans would fight on the left flank in Lorraine whilst the British struck eastwards through Cambrai. The swelling American forces fought hard and well, their numbers growing daily. Battering through the Kriemhilde Line to reach Sedan, heavy with history, cost them dear but it was taken nonetheless.

George Harbottle, after some re-shuffling of company officers, with his precious guns, was being moved southwards in June. His new comrades in 'C' Company were known as the 'gramophone' unit. This on account of the fact the commanding officer and second-in-command were both 'to put it mildly besotted about music'. C Company could boast 'a very good instrument with a large horn'. This prized possession was carefully transported neatly packed into one of the gun limbers (more usually reserved for ammunition) along with a fine classical selection: 'every officer who went on leave to England had to come back with a suitable record of equal calibre. The Misha Elman string quartet was very much to the fore in America at this period and we had many of their recordings.'

George got on well with his seniors, Major Hamilton, a Yorkshireman, and the Canadian Captain Rosher. Amiable and imperturbable, the captain was a thoroughly decent type though rather eccentric in his time-keeping. 'His morning rounds of the guns, as often as not were in the afternoon, and as he would go into great detail about any gun position and talk to everyone, he would often be having dinner in the mess at some hour nearing midnight...' George's previous experience with billeting arrangements and his relative mastery of French meant he was selected for this role as the company concentrated south of Doullens prior to the big move. His new mount, charmingly named 'Jessica', proved more than lively, attempting several times to relieve herself of her officer burden. 'I ... gave her a smack between the ears with my riding crop. She tried it again and got the same treatment, that terminated her antics and we lived very happily together until the day I was en route for England and demobilization.'

Billeting was a tedious and frequently difficult chore. 'We had to find accommodation for seven officers, the officers' mess, 50 other ranks and 40 horses and mules'. The company had to spend a week or so in these billets whilst the division made ready. Getting the men onto trains, regulation two score per cattle truck, usually proved quite easy. Mules were a different matter, 'mules are the devil'. The rail journey took 15th Scottish some 25 miles south of Compiegne to the village of Creil on the Oise. George's Company was to be billeted in Pont St Maxence, an idyllic location, untouched by war, with the broad sweep of the Oise running through.

It was time for cricket. The CO of 'D' Company, a Major Forester, had in peacetime been a fast bowler in the Derbyshire County XI. He had the kit and had managed to locate a suitable pitch. Volunteers for an inter-company game were urgently sought. George, a keen cricketer, and half a dozen other soldiers formed the nucleus of one team. Batting was opened by another county-level player, the aptly named Sergeant Bowley. Forester's bowling was deadly, 'Bowley being out, caught off his bat handle, when trying to protect his face, commented to me as he took off his pads that it wasn't pads I needed but a steel helmet!' Before George entered the fast bowler's sights, the war trumpets sounded loud and clear and the cricketing gear went back into a gun limber.

Such was the urgency, they moved up by motor vehicle, rather than with more sedate horse-drawn limbers. This was the time of Foch's first counter-stroke with the Germans now falling back towards the line of the Aisne, where they'd begun digging in during autumn 1914. As the Allied blow was itself running out of steam, the 15th Scottish would relieve the American 1st Division. The chase wound rapidly through a succession of townships, to the château of Vierzy where officers slept in the superb library, miraculously spared. Next morning they moved up towards the line where another château at Buzancy had not escaped the war. The Germans had fortified the place and it formed a seemingly immovable bastion anchoring their improvised lines.

At midday, the machine gunners grabbed rations just beyond a small river. George and his section moved forward, the guns sounding ever louder. The British were unprepared for the relative informality of their new American comrades and the rather casual handover. Their guide was fairly nonchalant but did point out a slight rise which was much visited by enemy artillery. With that helpful advice it was 'that's it chum, guess I beat it now – bye'. He disappeared, swift as a hare and the newcomers were on their own.

Not by any means alone though. Their own infantry were ahead and the overall situation was extremely fluid – to the extent nobody was exactly sure of anything. A diminutive copse some 200 yards in front was thought to be an enemy nest and about to be swept by a fighting patrol. The guns would give covering fire and deal with any targets flushed out. In the event there were none. The trees proved innocent of any foe. The Germans did not intend to stand. What C Company was facing was a determined rearguard, well dug in and supported. A very determined rearguard as it proved, for a fortnight's siege and seven attempts at break in did not budge them.

The machine gunners found the French maps upon which they were obliged to rely inadequate compared to British OS equivalents, 'pretty hopeless … small scale and without contours'. The next target was the formidable bulk of Buzancy. For the current British escalade, the guns would support the right flank of the assault. Happily, there were some aerial photos of the château to hand. C Company was not to advance with the first wave but to remain in support till the place was cleared, then move up and consolidate. At noon the signal came and George came forward with his two leading gun teams.

As ever in the fog of war, matters were not as clear cut as the optimistic message might suggest. Only part of the position had fallen. Enemy defence on the right was still holding up vigorously; 'the gap between our copse and the wall of the chateau was being swept by MG fire from a strongpoint on the right flank'. This was tricky and the gunners couldn't simply make a dash for it. If any of the team was hit then they'd be without a vital component or bereft of ammunition. A slight fold in the ground offered possibilities. The gunners now crawled forward, dragging their cumbersome charges. Only one man was injured. In front of them now, the solid park wall of the chateau, a dozen feet high, 'took some scaling'. Getting over with guns and gear was no mean feat. The men used each other as a human ladder, still under fire. Each climber straddled the rampart so kit could be passed up and over. At last, without loss, they were in.

A fresh challenge arose as they crept forward to find their infantry comrades, but there were none to be found. In fact the attackers had been dislodged and were falling back over open ground. 'I could see no officer anywhere and knew that a movement like that could develop into anything.' Spotting a tree line and hedge some 100 yards past the field, George sent two NCOs with a brace of Vickers to take firing positions there. Next, he found a sergeant from those Gordons who had put in the attack and instructed him to rally on the guns. This worked. Very soon the machine gunners and infantry had formed a workable defensive line, backed by additional Lewis guns and an abandoned German Maxim that was soon got into action.

His rally party swiftly attracted new members. At length several officers from the Gordons turned up and took charge of the thin khaki line. George's instructions were, the action over, to report to Company HQ. Here, his greeting was rapturous. The sergeant leading the section behind, seeing George's team vanish over the wall with the foot in full retreat, had assumed they were by now all dead or captured. George was already posted as missing in action. That night, the Germans withdrew leaving the battered château to the British. The place was empty, only the dead remaining: 'These attacks on Buzancy had been costly in casualties and while I was crossing the field when taking my guns into the chateau grounds, I noticed the dead of five nations: French, American, Scots, German and English.'

George won a Military Cross for his role in the attack on Buzancy and came safe home, married and resumed his civilian occupation. He published his memoir privately in 1981, though he wrote several other volumes on sport. He died at the age of 103. His name is on the roll of honour on the wall of the South Northumberland Cricket Club, where he played out his life-long love of the sport.

After the fight for Buzancy, the 17th French Division erected a memorial to the 15th Scottish. It reads:

Ici fleurira toujours le glorieux
Chardon d'Ecosse parmi les roses de France

Here the glorious thistle of Scotland will
Flourish for ever amid the roses of France

That pretty much says it all.

Black day of the German Army

War requires an ingenious mind, always alert, and one day the
reward of victory comes. Don't talk to me about glory, beauty,
enthusiasm. They are verbal manifestations. Nothing exists except
facts and facts alone are of any use. A useful fact, and one that
satisfied me, was the signing of the armistice … Without trying to
drag in miracles just because clear vision is vouchsafed to a man,
because afterwards it turns out this clear vision has determined
movements fraught with enormous consequences in a formidable
war, I still hold that this clear vision comes from a Providential force,
in the hands of which one is an instrument, and that the victorious
decision emanates from above, by the higher and Divine will.

Marshal Ferdinand Foch

One of the early casualties of Ludendorff's *Michael* offensive
was General 'Paddy' Gough. The failures of Fifth Army were
laid at his door and his head provided the requisite sacrifice. He
was replaced by Rawlinson, a general who, as Richard Holmes
observes, had learnt a great deal about fighting the Germans
since the Somme. Besides, the German Army, like the British
and French, was not what it had been two years or even a year
before. Ludendorff's gains had been won at huge cost. The best
and the bravest, as ever, paid the fullest price. What remained, in
qualitative terms, was simply not the same.

Having seen to his defences, Rawlinson came to the view that
the time was perhaps ripe for thinking in more offensive terms.

15th August, 1917.

No. 157. Vol 7.

THE WAR
Illustrated

A PICTURE-RECORD of Events by Land, Sea and Air.   Edited by J. A. HAMMERTON

PREPARING FOR THE LATEST "BIG PUSH." The British Commander-in-Chief and his leading generals Sir Hubert Gough and Sir Henry Rawlinson on his right; on his left Sir Henry Horne and Sir Herbert Plumer—before him the map of Western Flanders. He is engrossed in strategic plans for the Third Battle of Ypres, the opening phase of which is described on page 8 in this issue.

The Big Push: Gough, Rawlinson, Haig, Horne and Plumer, The War
Illustrated, *August 1917. (Author's collection)*

He could not conjure up more men but he could replace flesh and blood that had failed against the terrible killing power of modern weapons with automatic fire and steel plate; more machine guns, more tanks. British artillery performance had improved already in leaps and bounds. Tanks, those great lumbering juggernauts that had rumbled onto the scene in 1916 were, with the new Mark V, substantially improved, faster (or at least less slow) and more reliable.

Heavy bombers had made their appearance and the beginnings of strategic air power which would loom large in the post-war debate were stirring: 'London Wednesday [1 August 1918] an official report from the RAF independent force in France states that on Monday night our machines attacked the railway stations at Offenburg, Rastaff and Baden. Stuttgart and Solingen were also attacked. Three hostile aerodromes and numerous ground targets were bombed and subjected to machine-gun fire. All our machines returned.'

In a war marked by filth, squalor, constant attrition and a vast, unceasing haemorrhage, 'the knights of the air' seemed, outwardly to represent something more chivalrous, nobler, and more Homeric than mass slaughter on the ground. This was a fiction of course, encouraged by both sides' propaganda, war in the air was every bit as deadly. In fact, the average life expectancy of a rookie flyer in the war was six weeks, in combat this could easily be measured in minutes.

A series of generally successful large-scale raids led Rawlinson to believe the time ripe for a wider offensive. The Allied blow would fall along a front from north of the Somme to just south of the Amiens–Villers–Bretonneux road. Rawlinson had long been a believer in 'bite and hold'. Haig, as ever wanted more and deeper. He would have a significant superiority in terms of tanks, guns and aircraft. The burgeoning role of the latter would be significant. Security was paramount throughout. When the blow fell at dawn on 8 August, the Germans were caught out and seriously savaged. Rawlinson was to say 'we have given the Germans a pretty good bump this time'. Both the official German history and Ludendorff gloomily concurred. This was indeed 'the black day' of a German army that had fought so very hard indeed throughout four years of titanic industrial war.

The 'Black Day' led to the Hundred Days' Offensive which led inexorably to Germany's defeat. Victory was bought at enormous cost. British casualties in August 1918 amounted to 80,000. The various attacks of the Hundred Days in all cost 220,000 more. These came from a diminishing stock. Britain was bled dry, as was France and as was Germany. That summer was one of Allied advances and German withdrawals. The latter were never in danger of becoming a rout. Stubborn rearguards, as seen at Buzancy, shielded every backwards step.

Sergeant McGuffie wins the Victoria Cross

R. A. Urquhart was conscripted and posted to 5th Battalion, King's Own Scottish Borderers, in January 1918:

> Our training during this period was mainly drill, physical training and sport, the objective being to smarten us up and make us fit. One item I remember well was jogging around the public park most mornings before breakfast. When May [1918] arrived we were sent to Kelling camp in Norfolk where we joined up with other recruits for another KOSB Battalion. Here, we received our complete training for overseas and met up with the Sandhurst trained platoon officers who brought us to France.

Arriving in Boulogne at the end of July and billeted in St Martin's camp, Urquhart read in the *Daily Mail* of a debate in the House of Commons: 'One of the Edinburgh MPs, Mr. J. Hogg had stood up in Parliament and accused the PM, Lloyd George, of sending boys under 19 years of age into the front line. This was denied by the PM who also said that any boys under 19 years who were up in the line would be sent down.' Urquhart found this amusing as he was only 18!

Like countless thousands of Tommies before them, the Borderers entrained on the unimaginably slow French railways in the familiar cattle trucks and chugged slowly and in near total darkness northwards. Compared to the footslogging ahead, this would almost, and in hindsight, appear luxurious: 'From that day, I have no recollection of reaching any destination whilst up in the line other than by foot'. They marched from Kemmel to Steenvoorde and then to Hillebroucq.

Early August and the new recruits found their battalion at Wormhout. Here they were introduced to Sergeant Major (acting) Louis McGuffie. At the venerable age of 25, he seemed to them an aged Olympian; 'he brought with him our first supply of cigarettes and tobacco'. They moved up closer to the front via Poperinghe and Plotijze. They were assured their first tour 'would be very quiet'. Perhaps they wondered how many other fresh recruits had received the same bland assurance and how many had in fact been hurled straight into the inferno?

> On arrival I was surprised to see that the trench ran along the boundary of the communal cemetery – situated not far from the Menin Gate. There we were accommodated in dugouts placed between the graves. Since joining the 5th Battalion, the young lads were usually billeted along with an older member of the battalion. On this occasion, I had one by the name of McGregor whose perky sense of humour banished the morbid surroundings of our sleeping accommodation. At dusk we had stand to in the trench where I placed my Lewis Gun on the rampart beside a white wooden cross where Prince Maurice of Battenberg lay buried. He had been a Lieutenant in the KRRC, killed in October 1914.

At night the skies were brightened and illuminated by German flares and, by day, they had a view of the skeletal carcass of the once-splendid Cloth Hall. 'A few days before we left the cemetery we were informed that a supply of wines had been brought up from the cellars of Ypres and we were invited to bring our canteens to obtain our share. The connoisseurs amongst us were disappointed when we received our allocation which was Vichy water!' From the hollow shell of Ypres, the KOSBs moved towards Kemmel:

As we marched, or should I say trekked, down a road towards the foot of the hill [Mt Kemmel] it became clearer, and we were able to see what was around us. We found ourselves walking on what we thought were discarded greatcoats and tunics. Eventually, we became aware of the situation and realized we were walking over the bodies of French and Germans who had been killed during the fighting earlier in the year. The surface of the road had been flattened by vehicles and in several places only the buttons of the uniforms along with scraps of cloth were visible as if they had been hurriedly buried or just run over and pressed down. Near the end of the road, an arm with a gloved, clenched hand was raised up from the elbow as if giving a signal to halt. It was a ghastly sight.

Attaining the summit and strung out in a skirmish line, Urquhart was sent on ahead with a small group of officers, over the crest and down the reverse slope 'like a group of hikers on a morning stroll'. Their stroll was soon halted by sniper fire as they moved towards the position known as Donegal Farm (a particularly 'hot' sector): 'we saw a hedge on the left and ran towards it. It gave us some protection until we reached a cornfield through which we crawled until we arrived at the path through the wood to Donegal Farm. There we found many shall holes. No sooner had we jumped into them than shells began to arrive behind me. On looking back, I saw stretcher-bearers carrying a lad away from a shell hole I had just left.'

No further movement was worth even contemplating till night. Then, cautiously forward again. One member of Urquhart's section, blundering about behind searching for lost ammunition, called out his name. This earned both a swift rebuke and a German flare, arcing brilliant in the night sky; 'so I told him not to move. Fortunately, we were not spotted but I saw we were very close to the German positions'. They crawled forward into a shell hole occupied by one of their own officers and an NCO. Plainly, they could hear German voices. The NCO volunteered to seek reinforcements but returned empty handed. Another English battalion was behind but would not come up without orders from an officer. They were at length relieved and moved back into the line. Though there was no large-scale fighting to begin with, Urquhart remembered:

> The three raids I took part in. the first was uneventful as far as though my section was involved, we did not see anything of the enemy. The second raid was similar, without sight of the Germans but eventful in the sense that an incident took place that I've never been able to understand. Before leaving, we were told that a rum ration would be sent to us. An unusual thing to happen and the only time such an arrangement was ever made before I took part in any action. The rum never arrived, so when I got back, I made enquiries and the explanation was that the two lads carrying the rum were challenged by a German, dropped it and ran off!
>
> Of these the third was the important one and, on this occasion, it was a 'sacrifice' patrol to enable the battalion to take up new positions for the big day. It seemed that the whole platoon was taking part. I had another Lewis-gunner with me and shelled the trench which was divided in two sections. The sergeant told me to remain with him and sent the others to the far section. As soon as they arrived there firing began and our Lewis-gunners went into action. When the German machine-gunners fired we were able to see them and noted their positions at the foot of the ridge.

As the initial exchange died down the NCO advised Urquhart he was expecting a runner with orders for them to withdraw. This forward position was too exposed and the Germans ahead would very likely soon be reinforced. It was to be hoped the runner would arrive ahead of the enemy reserves:

> This, however did not happen, 2.00 a.m. arrived but no messenger. Sometime after this the Lewis-gunner in the far section resumed firing until his gun jammed. I had to take my gun along. To reach the other section I had to jump a wide gap between the two and, when doing so, I landed among a collection of tin cans. When I jumped back [having swapped the jammed weapon for his own], I managed to avoid the MG rounds that struck as I got across. The

firing continued and soon, stick bombs began to fall which made it impossible to remain. The sergeant decided we should get back. When we reached base we were told we would be mentioned in dispatches and that the cooks were preparing for us a very special meal. When it arrived we were unable to enjoy it as it had been sent up in petrol cans! The meal was cold rice pudding, flavoured with petrol.

On 29 September the Borderers went over the top at Wytschaete, sweeping forwards till halted by a German bunker whose occupants remained in residence. Despite this, a platoon of the Argylls pitched up beside and disputed their right. Sergeant McGuffie cut across the argument by winkling the remaining defenders out with grenades: 'it was enough; out they came, "Kamerad"'. Their next halt was in a deep shell-hole, where they were 'pinned down by MG fire coming from farm ruins a few hundred yards to the left. Fortunately, the shell hole was a very deep one which gave us good protection.' Sergeant McGuffie had acquired a good pair of German officers' binoculars as booty: '"There's some Boche coming down the road, let them have it!" I got the gun into position and asked for a look through the glasses. I saw a single file of figures at the top of the road, just coming out of the wood. In front was a German but I noticed that the one behind him was British.' These were now seen to be British POWs with German escorts:

We both got out of the shell-hole and McGuffie set off towards the gap in the wire. I presumed the prisoners were some of the A&SH – I was hoping they'd break away from their escort. They were about to do so when the Boche at the rear, who had a stick in his hand, touched the Argyll in front of him, indicating he should keep moving.

I then asked someone to pass me up his rifle. At the same time I said I could do with a bit of company so another lad came up beside me. The German in front took fright and went to his companion when we both raised our rifles. The Argylls then threw themselves on the ground and the Germans ran off towards the road. We fired and they jumped into a small shell hole where they remained until McGuffie reached them.

It was the Germans' turn to become prisoners and McGuffie re-distributed the loot from their pockets, much of which was the property of the newly liberated Highlanders. As the sergeant was doling out his gains, the platoon officer found them and advised that, as the company commander was down, he would have to take over, leaving the platoon in Sergeant McGuffie's capable hands:

McGuffie took charge at 2.00 p.m. and came back to the shell-hole 'come on lads, we have to join the rest of the company up the road.' For ¾ of the way up we had cover from a high embankment on our left which offered us protection from the MG we knew was waiting for us. As soon as we lost that cover and crossed to the other side of the road, the bullets arrived at my feet. After the second burst, McGuffie and the lad in front of me reached the wood and jumped into a trench.

It was at this point that Urquhart's luck ran out:

I was about to follow them when I was hit jumping into the trench. McGuffie came back to me and, handing me some field dressings, told me to dump the Lewis Gun and my equipment and get back to the MO. As I was doing so a Lewis-gunner shouted over to me that it would be safe to do so as he'd finished off the German who'd shot me.

For his attack on the blockhouse, rescue of the prisoners and assaulting several enemy dugouts, Sergeant Louis McGuffie was awarded the Victoria Cross: 'McGuffie deserved the VC. It is difficult to get to know officers and NCOs due to the high rate of change. At Wormhout he welcomed me into the battalion and at Quarante Bois he arranged for my departure. I shall always remember his coolness and disregard for the German machine guns when he stood on the edge of the shell-hole.'

Private Urquhart had his wounds dressed at the ADS, then transported on a stretcher to a base hospital at St. Omer where, after an operation, he was sent on to Boulogne. His wound was a 'Blighty' one and he convalesced at Harrogate. He was finally demobbed at Duddington camp near Edinburgh early in 1919. Sergeant McGuffie was killed by a shell on 4 October.

It was also towards the end of September that Fourth Army crashed through the Hindenburg Line, the seemingly impregnable bastion of German hopes. There were no more storm-troopers left. Ludendorff's offensives had cost his nation another million men. This was warfare on a scale never before attempted, nor even imagined. The ruin of the Hindenburg Line convinced the ever more pessimistic Ludendorff that this was the end for Germany.

He was quite right. October brought nothing but endless fresh defeats and costly withdrawals. The Allies, scent of victory now in their nostrils, bore on relentlessly, though at a continuing dreadful cost to both sides. By the start of November the British were back at Mons where, for the BEF, it had all begun over four years previously. At 10.58 on 11 November one Private Price, a Canadian, became the last Allied soldier to die in battle, a mere two minutes before it was all over, one of history's unenviable footnotes.

CHAPTER 6

REMEMBRANCE

1919

At every Great War memorial service, the soldier is referred to as though patriotism had been the chief influence that had made him join the army and ultimately die in action. To the ex-serviceman who has had his eyes opened to the lies and deceptions of the Great War, how sad and ignorant it all is, he knows that practically all the pious outpourings over their dead comrades and comrades enemies are based on a false thesis.

The majority of the rank and file of the 'Contemptibles' joined the army for many various reasons other than that of patriotism; unemployment, home troubles and petty evils were the best recruiting sergeants in pre-war days and, when the war came, the spirit of adventure was the main influence, backed by every possible means of enticement and coercion. If the psychology of the un-conscripted Great War British soldier could ever be written, patriotism would be the least of impulses and hard instinct of men of fighting temperament at the top.

The truth about the non-commissioned soldier, who fought in the Great War, is a thing to be ashamed of, instead of being blessed and glorified as a virtue by those who are far removed from the foul realities of it.

Charles H. Moss, Sergeant 18th (Pals) Battalion DLI (*c.* 1924)

War correspondent Philip Gibbs reported in his bulletin to the *North Mail* on 12 November 1918: 'Our troops knew early this morning that the armistice had been signed. I stopped on my way to Mons outside a Brigade HQ, and an officer said 'hostilities will cease at eleven o'clock.' Then he added as all men add in their hearts, 'thank God for that. All the way to Mons there were columns of troops on the march and their bands played ahead of them and almost every man had a flag on his rifle. There were flowers in their caps and in their tunics, red and white chrysanthemums given by crowds of people who cheered them on their way, people who, in many of these villages had been only one day liberated from the German yoke. Our men marched singing with a smiling light in their eyes. They had done their job and it was finished – with the greatest victory in the world.'

It was a victory, one dearly bought and one which led inexorably to an even worse war within a generation; that this was 'the war to end all wars', proved a bitter irony. The harshness of Versailles and Germany's shame would open the door for Hitler and the Nazis. Tommy would not return to 'a land fit for heroes' as he had been promised, instead coming back to poverty, unemployment, hunger and despair. His sons were forced to march again twenty years later.

Conscientious objectors

John's grandfather, James Sadler, was a stone-mason and regular chapel-goer. Though he'd left school when barely into his teens, he had a life-long interest in education as a path to self-knowledge and self-improvement. He was viscerally opposed to war, one of those early members of the Labour party who saw the war as being cynically engineered by the forces of capitalism. He refused to serve when ordered for conscription and wouldn't accept any compromise. He was imprisoned in Richmond, threatened with

Passing Under Arms Through Armistice to Peace

The whirligig of time brings its revenges in a town on the Rhine—a German officer crossing a bridge on which a couple of French sentries are posted.

Part of the seemingly endless procession of returning allied prisoners on the march from Germany. Inset above : One of the guns of the French battery at Mariakerke, on the Belgian coast. It is kept in position in case of any Hun attempt to break the armistice.

Going Home, The War Illustrated, *January 1919. (Author's collection)*

the firing squad and, when he went on hunger strike, force fed. His health was adversely affected, ruined and he was only sent home to die. He actually lived until the age of 70, though the scars of this ordeal – torture by modern standards – marked him for life.

Though the outbreak of war was greeted with patriotic zeal throughout Europe there were also many committed pacifists who refused to have anything to do with the hostilities. These objectors were few in number (Britain held about 16,000) and they had no impact on the number of Britons in khaki prior to conscription. The 'system' didn't like dissenters though; they were bad for morale, an incipient cancer that might spread.

Many 'conchies', such as Jim Sadler and Bert Brocklesby, were very religious. On the day war was declared Bert expostulated 'God has not put me on this Earth to go destroying His children'. Jim never went back to church after the day he listened to the minister, in 1914, urging all who could to volunteer and do their patriotic chore. The debate is still relevant today – does a citizen have the right, in the face of a national crisis, to put conscience above civic responsibility. In 1914, most would have said not.

> You'd leave me cold though this our arguing
> Endured till dawn, you lack the essential thing.
> Healthy and leisured, pious, gentle, learned,
> 'You feel forbidden to fight' and thus unconcerned
> With that vast horror which defeat would bring.
>
> Hence, tho' you touched of David's lyre the string,
> Or wrote with quill plucked from an angel's wing,
> Unless you 'gave your body to be burned',
> You'd leave me cold.
>
> 'You feel it wrong to nurse'. While others fling
> Red life in the scale, what is your offering?
> Levite! In you the milk of pity has turned!
> For if sore wounded, and with eyes that yearned,
> I lay in the Jericho Road a-perishing,
> You'd leave me cold!

H.M.W: *To a Conscientious Objector* (30 December 1916)

'Conchie' was the obverse of 'Tommy', driven by the same individualism and notion of a higher duty yet interpreting the path to follow very differently. They might, at the outset, expect the black spot of a white feather or some casual insults. As the war dragged into its second and third year with the body count rising dizzyingly and horribly, the conchie became a butt of oppression as well as derision. His cards were marked.

While enlistment remained voluntary, pacifists could not be said to be standing outside the law, merely the zeitgeist. When conscription was introduced in February 1916 all conchies had to appear before a military tribunal to explain why they believed they should be exempt. Most arguments fell on deaf ears; the mood of the tribunals was against them. One conchie was brusquely informed he 'was only fit to be on the point of a German bayonet'. Some agreed to serve in non-combat roles, a half-way house compromise. The conchie wasn't required to bear arms himself but man the logistical tail and back up those who did. This wasn't cowardice – those who served as stretcher-bearers were as much in harm's way as the average rifleman.

Jim Sadler saw any participation as aiding and therefore supporting war and refused to serve in any capacity. Some refused even to peel spuds in the line. It was these, the zealots, who were singled out for special treatment, thrown into solitary confinement and fed on bread and water. Some wanted these incorrigibles shot '*pour encourager les autres*', lest the contagion of disobedience spread.

Of those who refused to participate at all, 36 were shipped out to France. Once over the Channel, their fate was beyond the pale of civilian authority. There existed a very real chance of these men being tried for wilful disobedience, punishable by death. Under King's Regulations these men could be subjected to field punishment before facing their court martial. All 36 admitted that they had deliberately refused orders. The military court's verdict was clear: 'When on active service refusal to obey an order. Tried by court martial and found guilty, sentenced to death by shooting. This sentence has been confirmed by the commander-in-chief, General Sir Douglas Haig' It was afterwards commuted by him to ten years penal servitude.

Ironically, some serving Tommies had real sympathy for conchies. It is a truism of war that one's fervour for the cause grows steadily stronger the further back you get from the front. Some wrote to their families that they admired the faith and stance of the three dozen dissenters. In the event none of them served their full decade behind bars and most were out of prison by 1919. Herbert Asquith, former prime minister, is said to have been incensed that the army had gone behind his back by deporting the conchies to France when they were still in reality civilians, referring to their treatment as 'abominable'.

Frederick Tait was born in Elswick, Newcastle in 1893 of good Labour stock, his father was an activist and Fred inherited a socialist vision. His grounds for refusing to serve were not based on faith but on pure politics. He wouldn't kill fellow workers at the behest of a capitalist cabal. Some men were given hard labour. Fred Tait was sentenced to solitary confinement. His work was stitching mail bags and from the regulations he quotes in his diary 'one learns that if the prisoner did not work, his conditions would be even more rigorous than the norm'. Prisoners were allowed half an hour a day exercise with other inmates and they could meet together in chapel, otherwise it was a punishable offence to talk to one another.

Fred began his diary when he had been in prison for a total of 21 months. He had been put in charge of the Prisoners' Wants Book in the library and managed to take a partially used copy small enough to conceal in his single pocket, together with pen and ink, back to his cell. On 28 March 1918, he scratched his first entry. Over the page he wrote his 'credo': 'Only one thing shines clearly through the mental torture, the broken hopes, the happy and sad dreams, the disappointments of the past two years. That is my ideal…. For the first time in the History of the World a body of men of all sects, and no sects, of all races, of all lands, has stood before the Peoples and proclaimed that Love, Peace and Fellowship are greater than War and Death…'

Fred's sister Nellie wrote that 'he was released on health grounds and joined the Friends Ambulance Corps, a body which cared only for wounded who could not be patched-up to fight again…'

The lost

Joseph William ('Willie') Stones was a stocky miner, classic bantam physique, 23 years of age who had enlisted at West Hartlepool in March 1915. He was a volunteer.

On 26 November 1916, 19th Battalion, DLI, was positioned before the battered shell of Roclincourt. Though the sector was nominally 'quiet', much raiding and counter-raiding went on. The defences overall were in poor shape. It was at 2.15am that Lieutenant Mundy and Lance-Sergeant Stones passed Post 'A' on a routine patrol. En route to the next position, they were jumped by a party of German raiders and shot up. The officer fell mortally wounded and Sergeant Stones seemingly bolted back to the post.

He continued along a communication trench until he reached the hub of Bogey and Wednesday Avenues. He was picked up by the battalion battle police well to the rear of the action, missing his personal weapons. Sergeant Stones was accused of 'shamefully casting away his arms in the presence of the enemy' and of having run away from the front line. He was tried on Christmas Eve. Counsel for the defence was provided by Captain Warmington, an experienced and mature solicitor in Civvy Street.

Lieutenant Howes testified that as the alarm was raised he saw Stones in the communication trench. This was about 150 yards to the rear. As NCO of the watch – and this was crucial – Stones should not have left his post at the front. The officer could confirm that the accused appeared to be 'very much upset'. Howes could not recall if he still had his rifle at that point.

Important evidence now came from Private Pinkney who was in the command dugout when Stones arrived to raise the alarm. The accused had then expressed urgent need to locate the company cooks before they were overrun. It was in the course of this fruitless search that Stones became visibly unwell, having difficulty using his legs. He had been sick for some time.

Pinkney was with Stones as the NCO tried to find the MO but, very soon after, the pair were intercepted and ordered back by the battle police. Sergeant Foster on duty that night stated that Stones was exhausted and trembling and claimed that Lieutenant Mundy, when wounded, had ordered him back. Certainly by now Stones was unarmed and, when questioned, told Foster he'd jammed his rifle and bayonet crossways in the trench behind to provide an obstacle to pursuing Germans. In the divisional war diary Willie Stones is initially described as being in a 'pitiable state of terror' – the word 'terrible' has been deleted. Foster continued his testimony as to the accused man's state of near nervous collapse.

Captain Warmington, opening his defence, adduced statements showing that Stones had twice reported sick with rheumatic pains in both legs. He then showed that there was no hard evidence to support an accusation that Willie Stones had deliberately cast aside his rifle and that only one witness saw him without it. When he and Mundy were fired on, he claimed his rifle was loaded but he didn't fire as not only was the safety on but so was the breech cover (designed to prevent mud and dust fouling the action). He had not fixed his bayonet. It seemed Lieutenant Mundy's revolver was still holstered and that neither man, being on a routine patrol, had anticipated sudden attack.

In summing up, Warmington reiterated his previous points and insisted there was insufficient evidence upon which to base a conviction. Character evidence, all favourable, was then given before the tribunal came to a finding. Willie Stones was found guilty of shamefully casting away his arms in the presence of the enemy, of leaving the front line and running away. He was sentenced to death. On 18 January 1917, at 7.35am on a winter's morning lined with freshly fallen snow, Sergeant Willie Stones was executed by firing squad – a victim of war.

Shot at Dawn memorial at the National Memorial Arboretum,
Staffordshire, England. (Harry Mitchell, [CC BY 4.0 (http://
creativecommons.org/licenses/by/4.0)], via Wikimedia Commons)

His name, like so many others, did not appear on any memorial. It would take until the 21st century and a new understanding of the impact of war on the human psyche before Willie Stones and 305 men like him would finally receive a pardon. They have their memorial now – surrounding the 'Shot at Dawn' statue in the National Memorial Arboretum.

Lest we forget

Through all the land, in city, town, village and shire, the sad memorials rose, a mournful roll call of the dead, hymns to a lost generation. Yet all too soon, other names were added from the next war and are being added yet. A total of 956,703 British and imperial personnel died in World War I, more than half have no known grave. This was four times the number than had been lost in the whole of the Napoleonic wars, a period covering 22 years. Never had Britain and her colonies mourned so many. Before 1919 there were few war memorials, mostly in barracks. We can't really imagine our cities, towns, villages, even hamlets, without their shrines of mourning. Schools, colleges, workplaces all had their beautifully inscribed brass plates with the list of names.

Sir Fabian Ware was neither soldier nor politician. At the age of 45 he was too old to fight but became commander of a mobile unit of the British Red Cross. Appalled at the immense deluge

The Thiepval Memorial to the Missing of the Somme was built 1928–32 and opened on 1 August 1932 by the Prince of Wales and the president of France. It has been described by architectural historian Gavin Stamp as 'the greatest executed British work of monumental architecture of the twentieth century'. The ingenious memorial arch houses a series of panels on which are inscribed the names of 72,246 British and imperial soldiers who died in the Somme battles and who have no known grave.

of casualties, he felt compelled to find some means to ensure the seemingly endless plains of scattered battlefield cemeteries were recreated as monuments to the fallen. Initially almost on an ad hoc basis, his outfit began recording and tending all the graves they could find. As early as 1915, the work was given official status by the War Office and incorporated into the broader army structure as the Graves Registration Commission.

Encouraged by the support of the Prince of Wales, Ware submitted a memorandum to the Imperial War Conference and in May 1917, the Imperial War Graves Commission was established by Royal Charter. The future Edward VIII was appointed president with Ware as vice-chairman. The commission's Sisyphean task got underway after the Armistice. Once ground for cemeteries and memorials had been guaranteed, the stupendous job of recording details of all those dead began. By 1918, some 587,000 graves had been identified and a further 559,000 casualties were registered as having no known grave.

Three of the most accomplished architects of the day: Sir Edwin Lutyens, Sir Herbert Baker and Sir Reginald Blomfield – were chosen to undertake the work of designing and constructing cemeteries and memorials. Rudyard Kipling was tasked, as literary guru, with advising on inscriptions. Kipling, of course, had his own tragedy, *My Boy Jack*. He'd moved heaven and earth, pulled every string, to ensure his son didn't miss out on the great adventure, despite hopeless eyesight. John Kipling, 18 years old, was killed at Loos in 1915, his parents left with the guilt and engulfing despair.

Today the seemingly innumerable cemeteries, perfectly preserved gardens of remembrance, row upon row of light-coloured Portland stones, borders and walkways immaculate, are the collective essence of memory.

After the war, in the hungry 1920s, there was much criticism of the lavish fund-raising and spending on Lutyens' great ziggurat to the dead of the Somme at Thiepval. Many felt, understandably, that the cash would have been better spent on welfare for those veterans who were begging on street corners and pawning their medals.

The memorials speak of sacrifice and loss and yet also, almost perversely of hope, that somehow we may learn from that terrible harvest. There's very little evidence that we do of course. It may be that the Covenant – that unwritten mutual obligation between soldier and civilian is part of Tommy's legacy. World War I was the first fought by Britain where a true citizen army was deployed. Those who were primarily civilians and who would not otherwise have contemplated a military career rushed to join up as a collective act of civic responsibility. They came from every walk of life and they were not conscripted, they chose. All previous wars had been fought by a primarily professional army and casualties by comparison relatively low. Tommy was truly England's son who went out to do his duty in a foreign field.

Nobody can pretend that when he came back, broken in body and/or mind, he was well cared for. He wasn't, but there was a collective awareness of sacrifice; that the nation had to mourn its lost sons. It should have been the war to end all wars but dolefully was merely the begetter of quite a few more. All those war memorials would soon have fresh panels engraved. In the years since 1945, only 1968 and 2016 passed without UK servicemen or women being killed by enemy action.

Great War casualties didn't just occur on the battlefield. Untold tens of thousands came back ruined in mind or body or both. John's wife's grandfather died of his Great War injuries, or as a consequence of them, in 1946. He's not listed on any war memorial. But he was still Tommy.

SOURCES

The authors have drawn on research for their own previously published works: *Tommy at War 1914–1918* (London, Biteback, 2013), *Tommy Rot – WWI Poetry they didn't let you read* (Gloucs., History Press, 2013) and *As Good as Any Man – the Diary of a Black Tommy* (Gloucs., History Press, 2014).

INTRODUCTION

Kipling's *Tommy* was written *c.* 1890 and first appears in his 1892 *Barrack-Room Ballads*. *Victory Day* first appears in *The Queen's Gift Book – in Aid of Queen Mary's Convalescent Auxiliary Hospitals* (1920). Information on the early history of the Northumberland Hussars – 'Noodles' comes from H. Pease, *The History of the Northumberland (Hussars) Yeomanry 1819 – 1923* (London, Constable 1924) and T. L. Hewitson's *Weekend Warriors from Tyne to Tweed* (Gloucs., Tempus, 2006). Detail of structure and organisation, kit and training comes from many sources but a handy short introduction is No. 81 in the Osprey Men-at-Arms series, *The British Army 1914–1918* by D. S. V. Foston and R. J. Marrion (illustrated by G. A. Embleton). Kate Luard published her memoirs anonymously as *Diary of a Nursing Sister on the Western Front 1914–1915*, William Blackwood, 1915. The memoirs of Herbert Waugh are quoted by kind courtesy of the Fusiliers Museum of Northumberland.

CHAPTER 1

The poem by Chas Anderson is unpublished (as far the authors are aware) and is included by kind permission of Tyne and Wear Archives and Museums (TWAM.DBC.1845/362). The Pennyman memoirs (also unpublished) are featured by kind consent of the King's Own Scottish Borderers Museum at Berwick Barracks. The family home of Ormesby Hall is now in the care of the National Trust and features a wide range of Pennyman memorabilia. The short verse from *Plum & Apple*, the unofficial bulletin of the 2nd Squadron, Northumberland Hussars, is from the regimental archive now in the care of

'A Soldier's Life' and Tyne and Wear Archive and Museums. The recollections of the Northumberland Hussars are all extracted from the first volume of the regimental history by Pease (see above).

CHAPTER 2

The memoirs of George Hilton are reproduced by kind permission of the Trustees of the KOSB Museum; those of Herbert Waugh by permission of the Trustees of the Fusiliers Museum of Northumberland. The experiences of Robert Constantine and John Walcote Gamble appear by kind courtesy of DCRO.

CHAPTER 3

Quoted extracts from Charles Moss' unpublished account is included by kind permission of DCRO.

CHAPTER 4

The unpublished recollections of John Evelyn Carr are reproduced by kind consent of Northumberland County Record Office. Arthur Roberts' fascinating memoir is reproduced in full in *As Good as any Man – the Diary of a Black Tommy*, co-authored by the present writers and published in 2014 by History Press. Norman Gladden's account is extracted from his own memoir *Ypres 1917*, published in London by New Kimber in 1967.

CHAPTER 5

The recollections of George Harbottle are from his privately published account *Civilian Soldier* (Newcastle, 1981) and are reproduced by kind permission of his literary executors. The description of Sergeant McGuffie winning the VC is included by kind permission of the Trustees of the KOSB Museum.

CHAPTER 6

As before, the words of Charles Moss are included by kind permission of DCRO, as is the extract from Gibbs and the verse *to A Conscientious Objector*. The extract from the diary of Frederick Tait is by kind permission of family while information on the trial by court martial of Willie Stones comes from the excellent *Blindfold & Alone: British Military Executions of the Great War* by C. Corns and J. Hughes-Wilson (London, Phoenix, 2005). Every evening at eight o'clock in the Belgian City of Ypres, 'Wipers' as it was known to Tommy, the local fire brigade band sound the last post in memory of those who died in the Ypres Salient: men who have no known grave, 54,395 of them. They have conducted this simple but infinitely eloquent tribute since Sir Reginald Bloomfield's great arch was competed in 1927 (with a short interruption from 1940–44).

ACKNOWLEDGEMENTS

This book could not have been written without the generous assistance of a number of organisations and individuals, particular thanks are due to: Roberta Goldwater of 'A Soldier's Life' and colleagues at Tyne and Wear Archives and Museums, Jules Wood of the Military Museum at Carlisle; Ian Martin of the King's Own Scottish Borderers Museum, Berwick upon Tweed; Trustees of the Green Howards Museum, Richmond; Trustees and staff of the (former) Durham Light Infantry Museum and Art Gallery, staff of Durham County Record Office; the staff of Northumberland County Archives at Woodhorn; the Trustees of the Fusiliers Museum of Northumberland, Alnwick; colleagues at the (former) North East Centre for Lifelong Learning at the University of Sunderland; staff at the Literary and Philosophical Society Library, Newcastle; Anna Flowers and colleagues at Central Libraries, Newcastle and Gateshead, Clayport Library Durham, Northumberland Libraries at Morpeth, Alnwick, Blyth, Hexham and Cramlington, to Glenn Baume and colleagues of the Heugh Gun Battery Trust Limited. We are also indebted to Lindsey and Colin Durward of Blyth Battery, Blyth, Northumberland; Peter Hart and the staff of the Imperial War Museum Sound Archive; Richard Groocock at the National Archive; Amy Cameron of National Army Museum; the archive staff of the Defence Academy of the United Kingdom at Shrivenham; David Fletcher of the Tank Museum, Bovington; Rod Mackenzie of the Argyll and Sutherland Highlanders Museum; Thomas B. Smyth of the Black Watch Museum; Paul Evans of the Royal Artillery Museum; The curator and staff of the Royal Engineers Museum & Archives, Chatham; Peter Barton of La Boisselle Study Group; John Stelling, Anthony Hall and Henry Ross of North War Museum Project; Tony Ball of the Western Front Association and the Women's Library. Special thanks are due to John Dale, Tony Hall, Rob Horne and David Metcalf, together with Ruth Sheppard and colleagues at Casemate for another successful collaboration.

Every effort has been made to trace copyright holders for those individuals whose diaries and correspondence we have used, held in the archives listed above. We would be grateful for any information which might help to trace those whose identities or addresses are not currently known.

John Sadler & Rosie Serdiville
February 2017

BIG GUNS

ARTILLERY ON THE BATTLEFIELD

ANGUS KONSTAM

Over seven centuries the artillery piece has evolved from a status symbol to one of the most deadly weapons wielded by man. Using gunpowder weapons was initially something of a black art, but over the centuries gunnery became a science, a dependable method of breaching fortifications, or overcoming an enemy on the battlefield.

By the 19th century, most European armies had artillery units manned with trained gunners; Napoleon, originally an artillery officer, then took the use of artillery to a new level. Over the following decades, rapid advances in gun technology paved the way for the devastatingly powerful heavy artillery that literally transformed the landscape during World War I. The use of rolling and box barrages shaped how armies fought on the front lines and powerful naval guns dictated the outcome of battles at sea.

By World War II the range of artillery had expanded to include self-propelled guns, and powerful anti-tank and anti-aircraft guns. In this informative introduction, Angus Konstam concisely explains how the development and evolving deployment of artillery led to big guns becoming the key to victory in two world wars and a potent force on the modern battlefield.

ISBN 9781612004884 • £7.99 • $12.95

FIGHTER ACES

KNIGHTS OF THE SKY

JOHN SADLER AND ROSIE SERDIVILLE

Just over a decade after the first successful powered flight, fearless pioneers were flying over the battlefields of France in flimsy biplanes. As more aircraft took to the skies, their pilots began to develop tactics to take down enemy aviators. Though the infantry in their muddy trenches might see aerial combat as glorious and chivalric, the reality for these 'Knights of the Sky' was very different and undeniably deadly: new Royal Flying Corps subalterns in 1917 had a life expectancy of 11 days.

In 1915 the term 'ace' was coined to denote a pilot adept at downing enemy aircraft, and top aces like the Red Baron, René Fonck and Billy Bishop became household names. The idea of the ace continued after the 1918 Armistice, although as the size of air forces increased, the prominence of the ace diminished. But still, the pilots who swirled and danced in Hurricanes and Spitfires over southern England in 1940 were, and remain, feted as 'the Few' who stood between Britain and invasion. Flying aircraft advanced beyond the wildest dreams of Great War pilots, the 'top' fighter aces of World War II would accrue hundreds of kills, though their life expectancy was still measured in weeks, rather than years.

World War II cemented the vital role of air power, and post-war innovation gave fighter pilots jet-powered fighters, enabling them to pursue duels over huge areas above modern battlefields. This entertaining introduction explores the history and cult of the fighter ace from the first pilots through late 20th century conflicts, which leads to discussion of whether the era of the fighter ace is at an end.

ISBN 9781612004822 • £7.99 • $12.95

SHARPSHOOTERS

MARKSMEN THROUGH THE AGES

GARY YEE

-------------------------➤

Throughout history, the best marksmen in any military force have been employed as marksmen or sharpshooters, and equipped with the best available weapons. The German states made the first serious use of sharpshooters on the battlefield during the Seven Years' War in the 18th century. Some of these talented riflemen were then employed as mercenaries in America, where the tactical use of the rifle in wooded terrain was valued.

By the Revolutionary Wars, American riflemen were formidable, able to blend into the landscape and take out targets at long range. Their potential was noted by the British who began to train rifle units; during the Napoleonic Wars, the Green Jackets were the elite of the British army. The mid-19th century saw the development of optical sights, meaning that the units of sharpshooters raised in the Civil War were even more lethal.

The accuracy of German sniper fire in the trenches in World War I provoked the British Army to create sniper schools, manuals, and counter-sniping tactics. However, lessons were not learned and the outbreak of World War II saw almost all major powers unprepared for sniping or counter-sniping, meaning that talented marksmen like Simö Häyhä were able to accrue massive scores.

In this accessible introduction packed with first-hand accounts, sniping expert Gary Yee explores the history of the marksman, his weapons, and tactics from the flintlock era through to the present day.

ISBN 9781612004860 • £7.99 • $12.95

GLADIATORS

FIGHTING TO THE DEATH IN ANCIENT ROME | M. C. BISHOP

This expert introduction explores the world of the gladiator in Ancient Rome: their weapons, fighting techniques and armour. The cult of the gladiator is explored, alongside their less glamorous fates which more often than not ended in violent death.

ISBN 9781612005133 • £7.99 • $12.95

VIKINGS

RAIDERS FROM THE SEA | KIM HJARDAR

Viking raiders were feared across Europe for centuries, striking suddenly and attacking with great force before withdrawing with stolen goods or captives. Viking society was highly militarised, honour was everything and losing one's reputation was worse than death. This short history of the Vikings discusses their ships, weapons and armour, and unique way of life.

ISBN 9781612005195 • £7.99 • $12.95

Knights

CHIVALRY AND VIOLENCE | JOHN SADLER AND ROSIE SERDIVILLE

A short introduction to the world of the medieval knight, from the years of training and the weapons he fought with, to the tournaments and culture surrounding the knightly life.

ISBN 9781612005171 • £7.99 • $12.95

GREEK WARRIORS

HOPLITES AND HEROES | CAROLYN WILLEKES

Thermopylae, Marathon: though fought 2,500 years ago in Ancient Greece, the names of these battles are more familiar to many than battles fought in the last half-century, but our concept of the men who fought in these battles may be more a product of Hollywood than Greece. This book sketches the change from heroic to hoplite warfare, and discusses the life, equipment and training of both the citizen soldiers of most Greek cities, and the professional soldiers of Sparta.

ISBN 9781612005157 • £7.99 • $12.95